THE VALUE OF EXCELLENCE

by

Etta Wilson

THE ENCYCLOPEDIA OF
ETHICAL BEHAVIOR

THE ROSEN PUBLISHING GROUP
NEW YORK

Published in 1991 by The Rosen Publishing Group, Inc.
29 East 21st Street, New York, NY 10010

First Edition

Library of Congress Cataloging-in-Publication Date

Wilson, Etta.
The value of excellence / by Etta Wilson. — 1st ed.
p. cm. — (The Encycloped of ethical behavior)
Includes bibliographical references and index.
Summary: A discussion of the benefits of excellence and how to achieve it.
ISBN 0-8239-1289-2
1. Excellence—Juvenile literature. [1. Excellence.] I. Title.
II. Series.
BJ1533.E82W53 1991
179'.9—dc20

91-15130
CIP
AC

Manufactured in the United States of America

ACKNOWLEDGMENTS

Writing a nonfiction book has been a little like having a persistent fever. I never thought it would kill me, but there were times I wished it would. The fact that I did live through the writing process is due to much help from others. I thank them all but will mention only two:

My good friend Carolyn Wilson, who gave me access to the materials at David Lipscomb University Library.

My husband, Amos, who relinquished his computer and our weekend time together for so many hours.

Contents

CHAPTER 1

E is for Excellence

You've probably heard someone make one of the following comments:

Way to go!	Out of sight, man!
That's great!	You're unbelievable!
Super!	Awesome!
You're on top of that!	That's incredible!

We use many words and terms to tell people that they are achieving worthwhile goals or using their talents to the fullest. The words and phrases change with the times, but the word *excellence* has long been used to describe high achievement and admirable personal values.

Excellence pops up in many places:

- On a poster in a store window celebrating one hundred years of "excellent service";
- On a banner in the movie "Dead Poets Society";
- On the side of a florist's van;
- Over the entrance to a hospital referring to "excellence" in health care;

- In a book review;
- In a locker room.

You may have read that Bill Cosby and his wife gave each of their children a name starting with E—Erika, Erinn, Ensa, Evin, and Ennis—to stand for excellence.

Most of us have some idea of what excellence means, but the word can be puzzling because it is used in different ways. Which of the following would you describe as excellent:

- A white Bengal tiger
- A forest fire that destroys 3,000 acres
- An exhibit of Monet's paintings
- A dad who leaves work early to see his son's first ball game
- A 160-year-old redwood tree
- A Supreme Court decision supporting the death penalty
- The Sphinx in Egypt
- A score of 18 on the SAT
- A rock music star who refuses to buy drugs for his recording sessions
- A field of clover
- A program that helps teenage mothers finish school
- A bronze statue of a cowboy on horseback by Frederick Remington
- A student council decision supporting the principal's ban on smoking on campus
- A page from the telephone directory in your city

As you look down the list, you can immediately spot one item that everyone agrees is excellent—the score of 18 on the SAT. On the other hand, you feel confident that no one will call a forest fire excellent. And there is nothing unique or excellent about a page from the telephone directory even though it gives the number you want.

Bill Cosby poses with his daughters Erinn and Erika. Their names begin with the letter "E" for Excellence.

Some items on the list are the result of natural processes—the tiger, the redwood, and the field of clover. Few people would call a common field of clover excellent unless they lived in a desert area. The ancient redwood and the rare tiger are not so common. They may be beautiful and stir our admiration, but we don't use the word excellent to describe them. They are in no way related to human endeavor or inner values.

Other items on the list are also generally thought of as beautiful. The paintings of Monet and the bronzes of Remington inspire many viewers and are often described as excellent works of art. That is to say they stand out among other paintings and bronzes as creative efforts that have greater quality, strength, and appeal.

The items on the list related to human situations present the toughest area of decision about excellence. We all admire a father who leaves work to see his son's game, but it is not unusual enough to make us call him an excellent parent. And if he gets angry at the umpire and embarrasses his son, he should stay at work! However, if he volunteers to coach the team, donates money to buy uniforms, and never misses a game, we might think of excellence to describe his efforts.

Evaluating excellence in human situations depends on who we are and what we think is important. We know that smoking is bad for the human body, but if we are addicted to nicotine we are not likely to think that banning smoking is an excellent decision. We may oppose the death penalty until someone we love very much is ruthlessly murdered. Then we come to feel that the death penalty is an excellent law.

At this point we have clarified some things about the meaning of excellence: The word applies to something that is unusual or not common; it applies to things that involve human effort or skill; it somehow includes values that most people agree are good, such as beauty or kindness or justice. We shall be looking at these aspects of the meaning of excellence in the pages ahead.

Our notion of excellence is influenced by life experiences. The murder of a loved one could convince us that the death penalty is an excellent institution.

For a long time excellence has been discussed in connection with schools and education. Perhaps your last assignment came back from the teacher with the word "Excellent" written at the top. Teachers once graded students on a scale of E for Excellent, G for Good, F for Fair, and P for Poor. The goal of high achievers was to make all Es, not all As as in most school systems today. An E was the mark of having excelled or done more than required in a subject. This connection between excellence and education shows up clearly in the dictionary, where one of the definitions of excellence is "first-class."

The term excellence is applied to the best or highest outside the school as well. Sports and musical competitions often give a rating of "Excellent" or an "Award of Excellence" to the best performers in the contests. Businesses also discuss excellence, especially in recent years. They know there is a connection between high performance and financial success. They recognize that part of excellence in business involves integrity, especially if they want to stay in business.

In spite of seeing and hearing the word excellence and thinking you understand it, you may not use it very much yourself. You may feel a little uncomfortable if someone describes your work as excellent or says you have achieved excellence. Many of us do. It usually means that we stand out in some way or are noticeable because of some talent or extra effort or special deed for the sake of others. And standing out can be embarrassing.

In fact, the word excellence is supposed to mean standing out or being noticeable above the crowd; it comes from two Latin words meaning "to rise high" or "to rise out of." Through the years the word excellence has carried the meaning of being higher or superior or outstanding. The picture it brings to mind is of someone standing on a hill or looking down from a tower. The person's position puts him or her in plain view.

Being excellent has nothing to do with being physically taller or stronger, and it often means more than just an outstanding achievement. The meaning of excellence nearly always includes some inner qualities or strengths that make a person noticeable. You may be called a person of excellence because you have been unusually honest or generous just as often as for winning a chess or karate competition.

Sometime in the sixteenth century in England the word excellence came to be used as a title of honor. From saying that the king or queen was an excellent person, the people of the court began to refer to the ruler as "Excellency" or "Your Excellency." The title was applied to royalty, of course, because they were recognized as persons of higher status. Their personal virtues were not always so plain to see.

In more recent times the title "Excellency" is used for ambassadors, governors, and bishops and archbishops in the Catholic Church. If you happen to write the Secretary-General of the United Nations, it is correct to address him or her as "Excellency."

This practice of associating certain people with excellence merely because they hold a certain position tends to make us uneasy with being called excellent or calling others excellent. The concept of individual worth and equality is important in nearly all countries in today's world. Every human being is entitled to some measure of respect regardless of position or status. The most familiar and best-loved passage in the U.S. Declaration of Independence reads: "We hold these truths to be self-evident: that all men are created equal..." To elevate one person over another with the title or description of excellence contradicts our belief in equal rights regardless of race, sex, income, social class, or family. It also tends to make us feel snobbish.

However, the same spirit that insists on equality for all also insists that all of us have the right to make the most of whatever talent or ability we may have; in other words, we have the right to achieve excellence or to stand out. You can make the most of yourself in a free country. "May the best man (or woman) win" is just as important in our thinking as "All men (and women) are created equal."

The two ideas work together in making up our definition of excellence. When students hold an election for officers of the honor council, it is understood that several students may qualify or be equal in fulfilling the responsibilities of office. However, it is also understood that they will compete against one another and that only one person will be elected. Each student who votes must decide what qualities are best for each office.

De Gaulle's leadership of the Free French forces in World War II won him a special place in the hearts of the French people.

Each time you make such a decision, you are helping to lift one person above others. You are defining excellence, but you are doing it because excellence or the most excellent person is needed in that leadership role. This way of defining excellence is built into the basic framework of democratic nations. The underlying structure of democratic government as we know it evolved from the time when people decided they wanted a government in which excellence was based on individual merit and inherent personal qualities rather than on being born into a particular family or using money to buy a position. History has proved that excellence in government is more likely to result in a democratic system. The French people were better served by President Charles de Gaulle than by King Louis XIV.

This freedom to strive for excellence is very precious to those who have not had it. Over the years thousands of immigrants have come to North America because they believed they would find the opportunity to achieve a better life. People of many nationalities continue to come. The winner of the national spelling bee in the United States is just as likely to be from India as Indiana, and the state science fair winner may be the child of Vietnamese boat people.

We have made a good start in seeking the meaning of excellence. We know it refers to unusual achievement and worthy inner qualities, either of an individual or a group. We know it means being above the ordinary and may mean being in the spotlight to some degree, but it does not mean knocking others out of opportunity.

If people call you "excellent," it is okay to feel good about it. They may be telling you any one of the following positive things:

- You have some special talent.
- You were willing to compete.
- You worked hard.
- You did not use money or family connections to become outstanding.
- You did not treat others unfairly.
- You set your sights high.

Maybe it means you fit all of those possibilities. That is real excellence—with a capital E.

CHAPTER 2

School and Career: Finding the Way of Excellence

Think how many different things you do in a single day, not to mention a week or month. You may find "Excellent" written at the top of your accounting assignment; your volleyball coach tells you that you played an "excellent" game; your band director announces that the last precision drill was "excellent"; the supervisor at the grocery where you work tells you that you're doing an "excellent" job keeping the shelves stocked.

In each of these situations you have used different skills and spent different amounts of time, but the evaluation of your performance is the same—it was good work. The definition and requirements of excellence often change from one activity to another. Keeping a clear idea of those changing requirements is the big challenge in finding the way of excellence.

Being committed to excellence in all areas of life is a little like driving a six-speed car—you have to keep changing gears according to what part of the road you're on at the moment. Fortunately, there are signposts or signals that help us know what excellence is in nearly all areas. If you take time at the start to discover those standards and how they are determined, you are in the driver's seat no matter what road you're driving on. You can move confidently toward your destination of excellence.

In Western culture most people spend their lives after early childhood either in school or at some form of employment. Those two areas are the main environments of our waking hours. We have to consider the standards of excellence at school and on the job if we want to reach excellence.

SCHOOL

In the classroom good grades are usually an indication of high achievement. All of us want to know how we are being evaluated and what our teachers think of our work. We are almost as much interested in knowing how our classmates and friends were evaluated. The question, "Wad'ja get?" is heard a lot after tests.

Several things go into evaluating performance in the classroom:

1. The teacher's expectations of what a student should learn in the subject. Those expectations are a combination of what the teacher learned as a student, the teacher's past experience in teaching, and what others expect the teacher to require of students in that subject.
2. The performance of other students in the class. If you wind up in an English class with several students who attended a special summer session in creative writing, their background and interest will probably set higher standards for that class than in other sections of English. Consequently you may be expected to perform at their level. You will also probably learn more.
3. The requirements for promotion set forth by those in charge of education in the town, county, state, or province.
4. The importance of education in the country or nation. Such factors as what politicians think schools ought to do, the current status of the economy, and traditional practices in education in the area affect the standards of performance. For example, in the United States the

federal government has recently been more supportive of private and parochial schools, with the result that educational standards may vary more than in the past.

When you receive a high grade, it usually means that you performed well according to standards that developed from all those sources. In many ways the standards for good performance are surprisingly similar because of communication and mobility in the culture.

Regardless of how the standards are set, many of us have negative feelings about grades. Nearly all of us have received an unfair grade in some class. Perhaps we misunderstood the directions on a test, or the teacher changed the requirements during the course. In creative courses such as art, grading can be very subjective. What one teacher considers an excellent woodcut print, another teacher considers not very good. Some teachers emphasize how you do the assignments; others care only about the end result. When one human being (a teacher) grades another (a student), human communication and judgment are involved, and there is no way it can be a perfectly fair process.

It is also true that teachers tend to talk more about grades that need improving than about good ones, and that gives us a negative attitude about grades in general. Teachers seem to assume that a student appreciates a good grade at the top of a paper without further comment. But if the grade is not so good, the paper is likely to have marks all over it and occasionally something like, "You have not done your homework!" written in the margin. If an entire class does poorly on a test, they may have to listen to a lecture about poor performance and lazy habits. That kind of teacher behavior can really convince us that grades have little to do with excellence.

Many of us get a bad taste about grades from our parents, because they tend to emphasize them too much. From first grade on, they want to see the report card right away, and, like teachers, they probably pay a lot more attention to the grades

We need feedback from teachers and other students in order to assess our own performance in school.

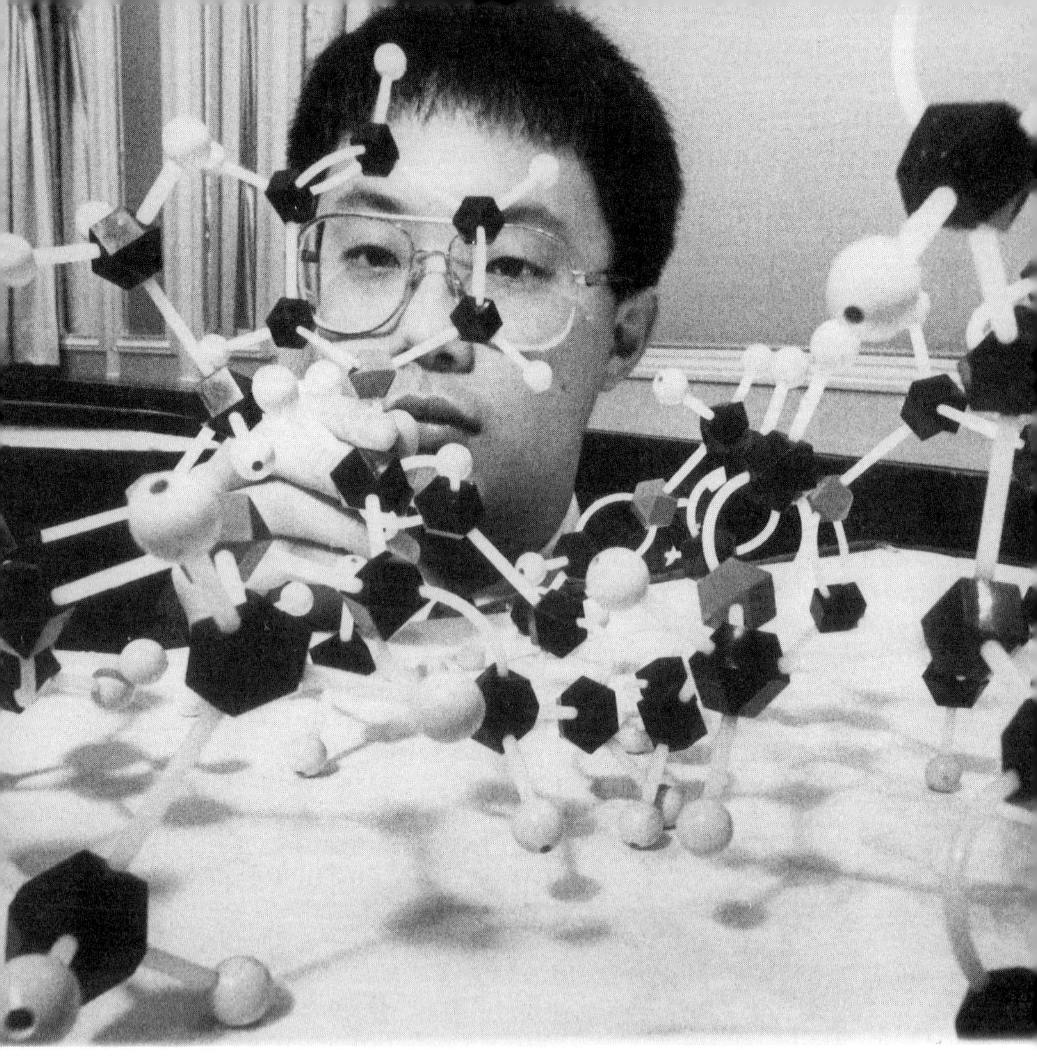

Hyoung Yoon Pash, 17, of New York City was one of the finalists in the Westinghouse Science Talent Search. His project involved synthesizing a series of complex new organic chemical compounds.

that are not the best. After a while we get the feeling that our parents like us less if our grades are not what they expect.

In spite of all these objections to grades, we know they usually indicate something about us, especially if we compare them over a period of time. If you receive consistently good grades, they tell you one of two things: you work very hard or you have a lot of ability or talent. Both may be true. (It is possible for good grades to show that you are good at cheating, but we'll discuss that later!)

If you have made excellent grades (in the top five to ten percent of your class) in science subjects for several years, you can feel confident that you have special abilities and knowledge in science. You have also probably studied your science assignments conscientiously. The more you know about science, the more you like it and become interested in scientific things outside the classroom. You start to watch the Discovery Channel on TV, to read *National Geographic*, and to visit science museums. Science becomes a more important part of your life. The good grades have helped you think of yourself as someone who is excellent in science.

And what would we do without grades? What if no one evaluated our progress in learning the skills and information we need to get along in today's world? We might go all the way through school with no one telling us whether we were doing well or not, or worse yet, have to grade ourselves. We would feel very uncertain and frustrated, because much of our self-image is formed by how we stack up in relation to others.

Most students must now take standardized tests to move from one level of study to another or to gain entry to college or other advanced training. Some tests are widely used such as the SAT (Stanford Achievement Test, developed in 1923) and the ACT (American College Test). Obviously your performance on such tests is judged against that of many more students than in a single class, and an excellent score may be harder to achieve.

Grades and scores on tests are the usual ways of evaluating performance in academic studies. However, we like more response to what we do than a number or letter on a report card. The more information we get from a teacher (whether a specific compliment or details about where we need to improve), the better we can learn. If Mrs. Jones says "Very good on the rebuttal" after you finish a debate in speech class, you go back over how you did the rebuttal and try to do as well or better in the next debate.

Such immediate, specific feedback is a big help in our striving for excellence, but it takes much more effort and time than a simple grade. It is almost impossible for a teacher to give that kind of evaluation to everyone in a class, although many teachers try.

We have looked at grades as a measure of achievement from both the student's viewpoint and the teacher's. We can agree that grades and grading are not perfect, but they are important. Overall a system of grades does help us define levels of achievement and our own special interests and talents.

The relation of grades to excellence is clearer when we look at the subjects we study in light of our larger goals. Striving for excellence as you go through school is somewhat like building a stone wall. The stonemason uses rocks of different sizes and shapes but fits them together to make the wall reach the height he desires.

Each time you start a new course of study, ask yourself:

How can this class help me to improve?
What can I learn here?
How does this class fit in with my goals?

Those are hard questions, and sometimes we have to be in a class for a while before the answers appear, but asking the questions puts you in control. They help you think of your education as a total process in which you are building something of real excellence—yourself.

CAREER

In the world of work the standards for performance have basic similarities from one job to another. No matter what you do, you are expected to give your time to the work and to produce the amount of work your employer has designated. In other words, you have to "show up and put out."

You may have to work at a job for a while to learn about how you will be evaluated and what is considered excellence. Most employers have a written job description for each position. For example, at a fast-food restaurant the cook's job is described, the counter clerk's job, the drive-through clerk's job. Besides what is on paper, the level of performance is determined by the manager's expectations, by the other employees, and perhaps by the flow of customers.

Many employers hire new employees on a period of probation, usually three to six months, to give them an opportunity to learn the job and see if they can do the work satisfactorily. Employers or supervisors also use job appraisals as a way of letting employees know how they are performing. The job appraisal often decides whether or not an employee gets a raise.

A job appraisal usually includes such factors as the following. The supervisor uses a numerical scale to grade the employee in each category.

1. *Quality of work*—Degree to which employee performs tasks accurately and on schedule.
2. *Initiative*—Degree to which employee develops better ways of performing tasks and seeks new responsibilities.

3. *Relationships*—Degree to which employee works well with others, treats them with respect and courtesy, and manages conflict so that it does not interfere with job performance.
4. *Reliability*—Degree to which employee can be counted on to observe company policies and procedures and to complete tasks.
5. *Flexibility*—Degree to which employee adapts to change and revised priorities and rearranges work schedules to achieve company objectives.

The job appraisal tells the employee what the company considers important in job performance, and an employee who achieves a high rating in all areas would certainly be considered excellent.

Some companies also ask the employee to set individual goals and then do a self-evaluation. The combination of the supervisor's evaluation and the employee's self-evaluation determines how well the employee is doing. The joint process helps a person to define excellence in the particular job he or she is performing.

Employers and managers have recently realized that other aspects of the work situation are important in encouraging employees to strive for excellence. In the book *In Search of Excellence* the authors examined a number of companies to determine why some were successful and considered good places to work. The major conclusion was that excellent companies have a basic philosophy of respecting the individual—both the customer and the employee. The managers of these companies want to help people work at their best possible level. They communicate often and openly with their employees about how things are going. Managers ask for ways to improve the service or product, and employees feel free to suggest improvements. The whole company seems to direct its attention to being the best at what it does, that is, to achieving excellence in its particular enterprise.

Sam Walton of the giant Arkansas-based Wal-Mart chain is known for dropping in at his stores and distribution centers to talk with his employees, whom he calls his "associates." He is described as having fun with the business, and people like to work for him. This man's spirit of enjoying work and trying to work together is a major factor in the chain's success.

That is true in any business—the person at the top determines the character of the company. If the company is to be a place that encourages excellence and top-level performance, it has to start with management. When you are looking for a job, look at the supervisors and owners if at all possible. Do they seem to like their work? How do they talk to others in the company? Do they mention helping you set goals? Do they describe your working relations with other employees? Sometimes we have to take a job to get immediate income, but if we don't like the atmosphere at the place of work we will probably be moving to another job before long.

The same things we said about grades as a measure of high achievement in school apply to money in careers. We expect more money for good performance on the job, but sooner or later it will not work out that way. Maybe there's a conflict with the supervisor, or the job description is changed, or the company has a bad year and freezes pay levels. There are many reasons why performing at a level of excellence may not result in higher pay. Excellence may even result in loss of a job if it makes the supervisor feel that his job is threatened.

Just as teachers and parents may focus too much on grades rather than good performance, the television and magazine ads focus on making us want money to buy the goods they advertise. The cars, clothes, compact discs, cosmetics, and concerts become so important that we think more about getting a raise than about raising the level of our job performance.

If we have been working only for money, we are likely to feel cheated when it does not increase as we had hoped. Unless you know inside yourself that you are a person of worth regardless of what you are paid, you may stop performing on the job. Or you may start to think that you are not very good at your job. But when your goals include using your talents or doing work that you really enjoy, you have found an extra payoff besides the paycheck. You have discovered the spirit of excellence, and it keeps you moving ahead—perhaps to another job!

In this chapter we have been discussing standards for measuring our performance in school and on the job. If excellence means being at the top, we have to know the standards for getting there. Those standards may change from one situation to another, so the first step in being a person of excellence is to discover how excellence is defined in the area where you want to do well. All through life we try new things, sometimes because we want to and sometimes because we have to. We enter a new career, take up a new sport, take a training course, or go back to school for another degree. In each situation we have to find out what is considered top performance.

That part of reaching for excellence can be called the outside part. The more important part is inside—the inner qualities of wanting to do our best and working toward that high mark. At some point we have to say, "Okay, I know what it takes. I'm going for it." Our desire and our persistent effort are critical. In the long run it may not matter very much who sets the standards (ourselves or others), and we don't have to have a

teacher or a coach or a buddy directing and encouraging us at every step—although it's a big help. The inner will to achieve and the day-to-day effort must direct us to excellence. In fact the way to excellence may be spelled W-O-R-K!

These inner qualities also include a confidence or sense of style and right performance. When we observe someone performing at the level of excellence, we often think how easy it looks. Gunther Gabel-Williams goes into the cage of tigers and makes them do their routines with speed and agility. But behind his graceful manipulation of the dangerous wild animals is a strong will and confidence gained from years of working with animals. He knows what is required for good performance, and he never loses his respect for the work or for those he works with—in this case, animals. He keeps the inner edge of excellence.

Working with circus tigers calls for boundless courage and a deep-felt respect for the animals.

CHAPTER 3

The Most Excellent Me

You have just received your midterm report card. You look across the rows for each subject and then down the column listing all the grades for months of work. You note that the grades are not all the same. You have better grades in some subjects than in others, and perhaps you remember the specific assignments that pulled your averages either up or down—a very good research paper or a low grade on a pop quiz. You may be surprised at some grades, or relieved and proud that you improved in a subject.

Although some people seem to achieve high levels of performance in many areas, all of us do better in some things than others. You may do excellent work in English but not in tennis; in history but not at the synthesizer. Our grades and scores tell us something about where we do well and where we don't. Grades and scores along with other kinds of evaluation we receive are important in helping us discover our strengths and weaknesses. This self-knowledge is the first step toward achieving excellence on a personal level.

SELF-DISCOVERY FROM OTHERS

The process of self-discovery is exciting, but it is not easy. The Scottish poet Robert Burns knew the problem well when he wrote:

"O would some power the giftie gie us
To see ourselves as others see us!"

Other people do see us in some ways more clearly than we see ourselves. Listening to what they say about us and noticing how they treat us is like standing in front of a mirror. We are able to see ourselves front and back, top to bottom. We get different perspectives from the viewpoints of others.

The reactions of our friends are especially important. When a good friend gives you a thumbs-up sign, you like yourself a lot better—and probably the friend. When your peers elect you to the Honor Council or designate you the nondrinking driver, you know they trust you. The signals we receive daily from our friends and classmates help us figure out who we are and what we do well. Psychological surveys have shown that the evaluations of peers during the teen years, when a person is first taking independent steps, tend to be accurate judgments about the person's abilities.

The first people who give us a view of ourselves are the members of our family. Your parents teach you your name and your body parts. They call you "smart" or "big" or "cute." If you have brothers or sisters, you learn about yourself in comparison to them. An older brother says, "You can't swing as high as I can." Your grandmother says, "Your hands are just like your uncle's."

If your mother let you help her in the kitchen when you were a toddler, encouraged you to read recipes when you could read, taught you how to shop for good produce, and let you plan special meals, by the time you are fifteen or so you would think of yourself as having some skills as a cook. You might be considering a career as a dietician or caterer or chef. A part of your self-image would be that of a person who likes to cook.

In that way our relationships with members of our family have great impact on how we see ourselves. However, family

ties are complex. Sometimes emotions get in the way, and family members cannot be objective. As we grow up we learn that some of what we picked up about ourselves was not accurate.

Guidance counselors and psychologists are more objective, and they use a variety of techniques to evaluate a person's abilities and personality. Most schools have someone trained in these techniques to test students and help them plan their curricula based on their strengths and weaknesses. A counselor may suggest that you take the Strong Vocational Interest test or the Myers-Briggs Type Indicator personality test. These tests do not give you a grade or rank. They simply describe you as a person, tell you your aptitudes or what kind of personality you have. In other words, they are another kind of mirror to help you see yourself better. The guidance counselor or therapist interprets the tests and your behavior. They may be your best friends in the process of self-discovery.

In addition to classmates, family, and people with special training in personal assessment, we look to coaches, pastors, priests, rabbis, scout leaders, camp counselors, and many others to tell us about ourselves. If they are wise and good, they will point us toward excellence as they encourage us where we do well, help us where we have shortcomings, and point us toward new goals to achieve.

SELF-DISCOVERY ON YOUR OWN

Alfred, Lord Tennyson, a British poet who was born only a few years after Robert Burns died, had a different idea of how we know ourselves and achieve excellence. In "The Palace of Art" he wrote:

> Self-reverence, self-knowledge, self-control,
> These three alone lead life to sovereign power.

If friends enjoy your company and seek your approval, it makes you feel worthwhile and good about yourself.

Tennyson knew that more than what any other person or test may tell us, it is what we feel and know about ourselves that makes the real difference in life. Ultimately your efforts toward excellence spring from within. Somewhere deep inside, each of us has an image of who we are and what we want to be. Our best efforts toward excellence take place when we are acting on that image.

Feeling that you can achieve excellence may seem just to happen. After many days of practicing the trumpet, one day you play that solo and suddenly it sounds as good as Al Hirt. The rush of pleasure, the recognition of your achievement is an inner signal that you have found something very worthwhile. It gives meaning to your life, and you begin to think of it more as fun because you feel so good about yourself when you are working to become better at it. "Do what you love, the money will follow" is a saying based on this approach to deciding what you want to achieve with your life. Or as the author Joseph Campbell advised: Follow your bliss.

For most of us the process of self-discovery takes a long time. Even when you have found something you really want to accomplish to the level of excellence, you have to keep discovering how to take the next step because you are growing and changing and because your environment is changing. You need some consistent means of evaluating your interests and efforts—just for you.

One way to discover more about yourself is by using written inventories or record-keeping exercises. Try completing the following sentences:

The thing I enjoyed doing most this past week was . . .
My classmates think I am good at . . .
If I could be anybody in the world, I would be . . .
Ten words that best describe me are . . .
I like to read about . . .
I spend more time doing . . . than anything else.
In the sixth grade my hero was . . .

It becomes a pleasure to devote hours of effort to something you love to do.

Completing these sentences can tell you quite a lot about yourself, and it can be fun as well.

Another way to use writing in discovering your areas of potential excellence is to keep a journal over a period of time, perhaps as long as six months. Buy a notebook, any kind from a simple spiral pad to one of the cloth-covered books found in gift shops and department stores. At the end of each day write down what you did that day and how you felt about it. You might want to include something someone said to you as well. For example:

Nov. 10
7:15—Overslept! No time for breakfast.
8:30– 9:30—Botany. We planted seeds that had come back from outer space. WOW!
9:30–10:30—English. Read poetry in class. It put me to sleep.
10:30–11:00—Activity period. Spanish club. I'm in charge of fiesta.
11:00–12:00—Geometry. I worked all the theorems except one.
12:00–12:30—Lunch. Ate with Joan. She said I need a haircut.
12:30– 1:30—Band. Glad to play something besides Sousa marches.
1:30– 2:30—History. Went to library to work on research paper. I need help!
2:30– 3:30—Spanish. 2nd year is more fun than 1st.
3:30– 5:30—Rode to swim practice with Jim. Instructor told me I would swim the 800 at the meet. I'll have to beat Susan.
7:00—Mom said Mr. Williams wants me to work durings the holidays, but I need to let him know soon.

At the end of six months or even six weeks of keeping such a daily record, go back and read what you have written. Ask yourself what you did best during that time and why. The patterns of your interests and abilities will be clearer. You should be able to write one sentence as a conclusion: "I learned . . . about myself."

Such record-keeping seems like a lot of work in the beginning, but it is very revealing. One day or even one week does not tell us that much about ourselves. In the example above, the writer seems to have a lot of enthusiasm for science and to like Spanish, to be fairly good in math and swimming, but not to care for poetry or history. After several weeks or months, however, the record may show that he or she is excellent in math and English, has given up swimming because the coach was pushing too hard, and has a good job opportunity with Mr. Williams.

One important part of this written record is that it's something you do by yourself. It's a little like talking to yourself about who you are. The daily routine of the writer above is full from early morning until dinnertime. And after dinner there's homework, TV, shopping, dates, maybe a job, phone calls. Soon it's 11:00 p.m. and time to catch some Z's for the next day. A whole day or week or month and soon a year has been filled to the brim with going and doing—but with no time to listen to yourself and think and plan what you really want to do and be. If you add one more item to that daily record, you can have the excitement of self-discovery:

9:30 p.m.—Wrote in my journal.

In just this way all of us develop ideas about who we are and what we can do well. You discover an interest or aptitude, you find opportunities to practice, and you move to a higher level of achievement. You set goals based on what you know within yourself. Those expectations in turn motivate you to new efforts to maintain the image you have of yourself.

ACTING ON THE IMAGE

The process of self-discovery is important, but as we said earlier it is only the first step. It may be tempting to spend all our time finding out who we are just as some people spend a lot of time looking in a mirror. That is particularly true during the teen years, when people have the first sense of independence. But if we never take action beyond self-discovery, we have missed what it's all about. We may also waste time going in wrong directions.

One of the most daring events in the winter Olympics is the race in which luge teams speed down a well-iced trough. Sometimes they ride high on one side of the trough almost perpendicular to the bottom, sometimes high on the other. They alter their position depending on the curve and the conditions of the track. That is somewhat like the way we move toward our goals. Sometimes we act more on what we have discovered about ourselves on our own, and sometimes more on what we learn from others. Putting the two together is a great method of reality testing—or going down the trough toward the finish line.

You may have a very clear idea of what you want to be, but you may not have tested it against your ability or examined the requirements for excellence in that field. If you want to be a tap dancer, you need some natural agility and a sense of rhythm. (You also need to practice and practice and practice.) It will become clear whether your ideal image is consistent with your abilities and interests. If it is not, you will need to search further for an ideal image or strength that is more attainable. What if Stevie Wonder had decided to be an air traffic controller and would not give up the image of himself sitting at the controls directing planes from the radar screens? His life would have been wasted, and we would have been denied a lot of good music.

Sometimes we fail to act when we find an area in which we are not very talented or have to admit that we are sluffing off. It is exactly at the point of discovering our strengths and weaknesses that we have critical choices to make if we are ever to be our best.

For example, let us say that John has always gotten good grades in math, and his aptitude scores show he has high ability in that subject. He really has two choices:

Actor and dancer Gregory Hines checks out the moves of this aspiring young tap dancer.

1. He can coast along in math class, making fair grades with little effort and without any clear goals related to his great potential.
2. He can work harder than ever in math because he enjoys it and knows he has great opportunity to excel.

The same choices present themselves in reverse when we discover our areas of weakness: We can avoid or ignore the area because it takes so much effort, or we can do extra work because we are determined to overcome the weakness. Those choices take courage, but if we want to stay in control of our lives, we must make them.

Many of us choose to work hard in a particular area for reasons that have little or nothing to do with our natural abilities. Perhaps you are trying to excel in a certain area because you want to make the top ten percent in your class; you want to earn an athletic letter; you want to buy a car. Those rewards can be powerful motivators for top performance, but they may not be realistic in light of your strengths.

If you have an after-school job at a boutique and you want to work full time for the summer, you will make sure that you perform well. You will get to work on time, you may offer to put in extra hours on Saturday, you won't take personal phone calls unless they are emergencies. You will keep the merchandise in good order and be courteous to customers and other staff. In other words, you will do everything you can to perform at the highest level because you want a full-time job and more pay. All this may or may not be related to any special talents you have in merchandising. You are acting on a short-term motivation rather than self-knowledge.

Sometimes we strive for excellence because we want to please others. Perhaps you had a favorite teacher in elementary school. He or she had a lot of enthusiasm and often told you that you were doing well. You knew that teacher really cared about you. By the end of the year you were studying hard and doing well because you liked the teacher. In such cases our actions turn out to be for our best interests as well.

Stevie Wonder recognized and acted upon his musical abilities from a very early age.

A whole group of people can adopt a mutual goal for the sake of another. Recently a football team determined to win the division championship in honor of their former team captain, who had been killed just as the season began.

We can find many rewards in reaching for personal excellence, but the rewards that count are the ones that come from knowing you have attained the highest level you could while treating others fairly. Mark Twain described the hunger for self-approval as the Master Passion. This inner sense of having done your best is a personal achievement with three aspects: You have looked at the mirror of what others think you can be, you have searched yourself to discover your own inner image, and you have acted in realistic ways to reach the highest possible goal.

In the recent time-warp movie "Bill and Ted's Excellent Adventure," the last scene depicted Abraham Lincoln saying to Bill and Ted, "Be excellent to one another." That sounds at first like a wrong use of the word, but the scriptwriter understood that personal excellence involves treating one another with respect as well as being creative and energetic in doing a history assignment. That is the final pat on the back of becoming excellent.

CHAPTER 4

Excellence Outside and In

Here are headlines from a recent morning newspaper: "Former president's diaries to be admitted as evidence in Iran/Contra affair." "Reports cited by mayor to council do not exist." "Phys Ed teacher leads double life as bank robber." "High school star quarterback plea-bargains rape charge." One day's news tells the story—people from the national level to the local community are having difficulty with the basic rules for living in human society.

In preceding chapters we have explored the meaning of excellence mostly from the individual's perspective. We have talked about how to discover the meaning of excellence in different areas of performance, and how to discover individual strengths and goals to develop as a person of excellence. The path of excellence definitely requires each of us to make the most of our particular talents in light of our life situation.

However, we do not live alone. We work with other people, we count on them for help, and we are often put in situations where we must compete with them. How you interact with others in these situations will in the long run determine your capacity for excellence. Someone may have great ability at stealing hubcaps and persist at it until he does it with great style and ease, but he will not be recognized for excellence!

Most of us understand excellence enough to know that it never involves criminal or destructive acts. The word would never come to mind in connection with murder or child molestation. But within the bounds of law-abiding behavior, our treatment of others may range from sneaky and self-centered to honest and kind. How we act within that range determines whether or not we can reach the goal of excellence over time.

In this chapter we shall look at two qualities that involve a person's interactions with others: integrity and respect. They are different in several ways from the inborn skills and talents or personal interests required to reach the level of excellence, but they are equally necessary.

INTEGRITY

As a review of the headlines above showed, the quality of integrity seems to be in short supply in our world, even among people who otherwise have a great deal going for them. Why does a talented athlete like Pete Rose become involved in gambling and jeopardize his chances for the Baseball Hall of Fame?

But we don't have to read the newspapers to see a lack of truth in the words and actions of other people. Perhaps your sister gets a call she doesn't want to take and asks you to say she's not at home. You have two friends who routinely cheat on tests in math class. The big guy on the intramural team jabs you in the ribs and then tells the referee he didn't do it. "Truth is the cry of all, but the game of the few," an author named George Berkeley wrote in 1744. He could just as easily have been talking about the present day.

Why is there this great tendency to shape our words and actions on standards other than honesty and fairness? It may seem at first like the easy way out or a shortcut, but it is a hard act to keep up. If I say something that isn't true, I have to remember what I said and to whom. Then I have to think whom that person might have told so that I can keep the lie going with them as well. From the moment I start this deception I am a divided person—one who knows the reality and one who knows the lie. More than that, I know that I have lied. I have to live with the stress of deception.

Former Cincinnati Reds manager Pete Rose walks with his head down through a crowd of media people on his way to the federal court.

If we continue the practice of shading the truth between what we say and what we do, we usually wind up deceiving ourselves more than anyone else. We start believing our own falsehood. It becomes a way of life. But truth like murder will out, as the proverb says. Other people are not stupid. They catch on sooner or later, even though they may not let us know that they are onto our act. They will probably tell others about our charade, but they let us go along thinking we have covered our tracks. It is as though an actor were on stage fully believing that he was the character in the play while the audience knew both the name of the character and the name of the actor.

Once we have started presenting ourselves as something we

are not (usually as better than we are), it is hard to stop—for several reasons. First, we want to be liked. We may have talent and ability, but we know we are not perfect or we suspect that we lack some quality that is important to someone we want to impress. We become anxious about being ignored or, worse yet, put down. What others think of us is really important, so we try to look our best—in more than just the clothes we wear. I drive my mom's new car in hopes that my friends will think it's mine. I say I have to work the night of the prom, but the truth is that I can't get a date. I am not breaking the law or really hurting anybody with these deceptions, but I am not really being truthful either. Wanting to be liked has tempted me to play a part.

A second reason that we may be dishonest is to avoid conflict with others. If we know that the truth is not what someone wants to hear, if someone will be upset or angry or make us feel quilty, we feel it is for both our interests to shade the truth a bit. Think how you would respond in these situations:

1. Your mom wants to know what time you got in last night, and it was a half hour after she told you to be home.
2. Your new coach wants to know your extra point percentage last year, and it was just under fifty percent.
3. Your dad asks if any of your friends use illegal drugs.
4. Your best friend wants to borrow your new shirt when you haven't worn it yet.

In each of these situations and hundreds like them, we don't want to go through the hassle that is likely to come from telling the truth or expressing our honest feelings. We can probably get by with a little deception and it's so much easier than a big scene, so we either lie or say something with several possible meanings.

A third reason we are not always honest is the pressure we

TV evangelists Jim and Tammy Bakker misled the viewing public by diverting large amounts of PTL money for their own benefit.

are under to succeed. It is so important to us to get that new job or make the team or be elected to the student council or get into the right college. There are so many things to buy and places to go. We've got to get ahead and make money, and so we lie about our abilities or past records.

We often see this kind of dishonesty in resumés. A person applying for a job wants to present himself in the best possible light, and employers expect applicants to select their best achievements. In presenting themselves on paper, however, they may use words that give an impression of something much greater than what actually happened. They figure they can fake it after they get the job—and maybe they can for a while.

Such dishonesty in the form of misrepresentation is prevalent in politics where the need to succeed—i.e., to be elected—is so strong. The Watergate scandal that led to the resignation of former President Richard M. Nixon in 1973 is an example of one deception building on another to the point of major corruption. Three years later, in the 1976 presidential campaign, the issue of integrity in government was still so important to voters that Jimmy Carter could use as a slogan, "I'll never lie to you." Even more shocking is the same kind of lying about personal behavior by television evangelists because we expect them to be trustworthy.

The role of television in revealing truth, especially about the character of public figures, is still being debated. Some like newswoman Diane Sawyer hold that because television gives a visual picture of the person we get a more complete picture. We can see the body language while we hear the words and thus make a more accurate judgment about the person's integrity. "What you see is what you get."

Others present evidence that because television is basically an entertainment medium, it both encourages people to play a role and encourages the viewer to expect a role-player. In other words, the very nature of television programming tends

TV evangelist Jim Bakker is escorted by a federal marshal, after being sentenced to 45 years in prison and fined $500,000 for fraud and conspiracy.

to downgrade the possibility of truth. "The medium is the message," was the way this view was expressed by social scientist Marshall McLuhan in 1964. As you watch television, ask yourself what level of honesty you expect from different types of programs. Does your opinion of the person on the screen as either trustworthy or untrustworthy affect the way you accept what is said?

On a more personal level, we need to ask ourselves how our behavior is affected by television. Perhaps we see performers only as performers, but after watching a few of them consistently we may begin to act like them in certain ways. That is not necessarily bad. We all need models and heroes, and we all have a public role to play. "All the world's a stage, . . . And one man in his time plays many parts," Shakespeare wrote in *As You Like It*. The question is how to "play our part" for the right reasons. Watching too much television, especially entertainment programs such as sitcoms and MTV, we tend to pick up styles and mannerisms that may not be true to who we are or effective for reaching our goals. We label people who try to act like others "fakey," and we have all seen them. They have spotlight fever.

Regardless of why we are not truthful, we cannot find the way of excellence so long as we are deceiving others and ourselves. Every time we misrepresent something on the outside, it does something to us on the inside. Most of us do intend to tell the truth, but honesty requires more than an intention. It includes all those things we do or think or say. If those things match one another and fit together like the pieces of a puzzle to make a true picture, we are not divided into what we intend and what we are. We are whole. In math an integer is a whole number; it is not divided. The Latin word *integer* is the root of integrity, meaning whole or complete or solid in moral character, the same outside as in, trustworthy. Personal integrity forms the core of excellence.

RESPECT FOR OTHERS

Another inner quality of excellence goes by different names. Some call it respect for others, some call it fair play, some call it

Under the Geneva Convention this group of American prisoners of war expected a certain standard of humane treatment in their captivity.

justice or equity. Whatever we name it, we are defining the words and actions that spring from a person's belief that all human beings have value and rights, that they cannot be used as objects for personal gain.

We can become very self-centered as we strive for success. We may have figured out what we do best, and we know others are counting on us to achieve it. There will certainly be those who have things we need or control over situations that are important to us in our striving for excellence. Throughout

history mankind has been prone either to forget the rights of others or to purposely deny those rights in search of personal gain. Nearly all of us put our personal freedoms at a higher priority than the rights of others.

The need for both justice and liberty in human interaction has resulted in a variety of rules and legal systems, ranging all the way from National Boxing Commission regulations to the Geneva Convention of 1864 governing the humane treatment of prisoners of war and of the sick and wounded in battle. As far back as the eighteenth century B.C. the Babylonian king Hammurabi instituted a legal code dealing with criminal and civil matters. The laws of the ancient Hebrews as laid down by Moses are found in the Old Testament, their simplest form being the Ten Commandments. Roman law developed for about ten centuries and spread throughout the provinces before it was codified by the Byzantine ruler Justinian I.

The Magna Carta, often called the most important instrument of English constitutional history, limited the personal power of the ruling monarch. When the English barons forced King John to sign the charter in 1215, he had to guarantee them certain privileges and protections. In other words, the rights of people living in the land were more important than the personal freedom of the king. The legendary hero Robin Hood tried to right some of the wrongs against the common people of that age with his band of merry men in Sherwood Forest, although he operated outside the law in many instances.

In modern times we are more familiar with the Bill of Rights of the United States Constitution and the laws that govern the state and community where we live. I may prefer driving on the left side of the road as they do in Britain, but if I use the public roads in the United States and want to avoid being injured or killed, I have to drive on the right.

None of us would argue against obeying the laws if we wish to achieve excellence. Obvious aspects of excellence are knowledge of the laws that govern human conduct and understanding of the principles of respect and equality upon which they are based. Most of us start to learn these laws at a fairly early age, and we also soon learn that the law cuts both ways. It may inhibit my freedom today, but it will protect my freedom tomorrow.

The crew of this catamaran work as a team to win a race in the America's Cup competition.

The way of excellence, however, goes beyond mere knowledge and obedience of laws and rules. Each of us has two basic needs that are in some ways opposed to each other. First, you need to feel good about yourself; you need to be outstanding or know that you have value as a unique person. At the same time you need to be a part of something larger than yourself; to be on a team or in a group or a community that is achieving something together.

In meeting the first need you are looking out for yourself, but to meet the second you must think of the good of the group. If you put all your energies into making the most of yourself, you will be a very lonely person and perhaps lose the help of others at an important point in your efforts. If you do everything for the team or group, you will wind up feeling used or not worthwhile as a person.

To live at the level of excellence means finding that balance between self-interest and the interests of others. The French Revolutionists of 1791 adopted the word *fraternité*, meaning brotherhood, to describe this necessary compromise between liberty for the individual and equality for all. We can sum it up simply in the words of Jesus known as the Golden Rule: "Do unto others as you would have them do unto you."

CHOICES—ALWAYS CHOICES

These inner qualities of excellence—integrity and respect for others—are very much matters of personal choice. You may have been born with great musical ability or high intelligence or good coordination and strength, any one of which you can develop to the point of high achievement in the appropriate field, but you are not born with the ability to tell either the truth or a lie, to respect other people or to cut them down.

It is true that you may have learned some bad ways of behaving from others, but no one forces you to keep on acting and talking that way. Those are choices you make every day, and although they are all within the range of law-abiding behavior, they can be very tough. For example:

- Do you call the human services department when you know the child in the apartment next door is being abused?
- Do you let a friend copy your homework?
- Do you congratulate the guy who beat you in tennis when you blew a game you should have won?
- Do you borrow an ID card to buy beer when you're the only one in your group under the legal age?

Coming down on the side of integrity and respect for others in situations like these is not easy. It takes courage because we are nearly always free to make the wrong choice and because there are so many voices around us trying to tell us what to do—often pushing us in opposite directions.

Each time we make a choice in our relations with others, we have to fall back on some inside code about what makes things fair or right in human society. John Rawls, a philosopher at Harvard University, has developed an interesting method of picking out those principles. He calls it the "veil of ignorance." He says that we can make the fairest decisions or rules about how to treat people if we assume that we don't know anything particular about ourselves, either who we are or who we will be:

- If I don't know whether I am male or female, I will act in ways that are fair to both.
- If I don't know whether I am white, black, Oriental, or Hispanic, I will act in ways that are fair to all.
- If I don't know whether I am living in an urban housing project, a middle-class suburb, or on a farm, I will pick an economy that is fair to all.
- If I don't know whether I will be a Catholic, Protestant, Jew, or Muslim, I will speak in ways that respect the religious convictions of all.
- If I don't know whether I will be six feet or four feet eight inches tall; weigh one hundred ninety or one hundred ten; use my right hand predominantly or my left; be diabetic, or paraplegic, or epileptic, in all cases I will choose ways of acting and speaking that are fair to all.

This method gives us a way of choosing that will be fair to us as well as others, of finding the balance. At the same time it helps us establish a code for future choices.

Many men and women through the ages have detemined that the best design for humans' treatment of one another comes from their religious faith. As they have developed a relationship with God, they have been able to see others as more valuable. They may start simply by adopting the code of behavior advocated by their religion's teaching, but as their knowledge and faith increase they move to a higher perspective of charity and self-sacrifice. It is paradoxical but continually proven true that when a person believes he or she is of value to a supernatural being, that person is enabled to care more for others. The sense of what is important, of how to make choices, has been radically changed.

A good analogy would be loading a personal computer with the basic program on a hard disc. Then no matter what software was loaded, the computer could perform. It would have the capacity to deal with the little questions because it had been loaded with the authority to manage the data received.

The character Tevye in "Fiddler on the Roof" may have said it best: "Because of our tradition, everybody knows who he is and what God expects him to do."

Making these daily choices for honesty and fairness is both the hardest and the easiest part of attaining excellence. As we have indicated, the choices are often difficult and require the development of some inner code. But the good news is that, in contrast to talents and skills that we may not have inherited or had the opportunity to acquire, we can control these choices. You will never reach excellence without making moral choices, but no one can stop you from making them. In that sense, excellence is everyone's reachable goal. As Mark Twain put it, "Always do right. This will gratify some people, and astonish the rest."

CHAPTER 5

Who Are Your Mom and Dad—and Does It Matter?

In our efforts to achieve excellence, there are times when life just doesn't seem fair. It is not hard to look around and see that some people have much more going for them. Your classmate Julie Smith has so much energy; she's always bouncing and smiling and trying new things. Jeff Scott's dad gave him a new car and he can drive to track practice every afternoon. That's a lot easier than having to catch the bus or subway at rush hour. And Jason Green is built like a tank—no wonder he got the first-string tackle slot. He'll probably wind up on a pro team like his older brother. Yes sir, some guys get all the breaks!

We are taught that everyone in a democratic society has equal rights and opportunity, but all of us know people who seem to have a head start, and that head start usually came from their family in one way or another. In our search for what excellence means and how to strive for it, we have to look at our families. Do they make a difference? If so, how?

FAMILY TIES IN HISTORY

Until fairly recent times most human societies have been based on hereditary privilege. A man, a woman, and their children have always formed the basic unit in human culture. The unique traits and characteristics of those individuals and the way they live from day to day are passed on from generation to generation. As time passes, other people who know that family develop expectations about them: All the men are tall, some of the family are short-tempered, they tend to buy land and settle in one area, they are skillful at growing vineyards. Thus the place a family occupies in the society becomes fixed to some degree, socially, geographically, and economically, and anyone born into that family is expected to be like the family.

The expectations that a person's life should be like that of the family were very strong in the past. They applied to the person's status, occupation, choice of a spouse, participation in government, and such lesser matters as where to sit at public events and what clothes to wear. Life was simpler because there were so few choices, but it was also restricted for any member of the family who might have wanted to do something different.

Royal families are a good example of these expectations and roles. Prince Charles is the oldest son in the royal family of Windsor. His mother is the Queen of England, and everyone expects him to inherit the throne. He has great privileges and power and wealth. However, he also has many functions to perform and very little family privacy.

The excessive influence of the family on a person's life began to decrease about three hundred years ago because of other things that were happening in the Western world. The Industrial Revolution emphasized a person's ability to produce goods or to devise ways to do work faster with the help of machines. Many people left the towns and villages where their

In spite of his privileges, Prince Charles has many demands on his time and is constantly in the public eye.

families had always lived to work in the large manufacturing cities. For them, it was the difference between depending on unreliable weather for a good crop and working for a sure wage in a factory.

It also meant living in a place where the family was not known. So the chief means of identity was whatever the person could accomplish on his own, not the family's reputation. The great migrations of people in search of better economic conditions and political freedom decreased the role of family in what a person could do with his or her life. Hard work and creative thinking were more important than remaining in the ancestral home place.

At about the same time, certain religious ideas were emerging in Europe that put strong emphasis on the value of each person in the order of society. Those convictions encouraged people to overthrow oppressive rulers, either in government or the church, and to insist on their individual rights. The ideas of individual rights and equality had taken firm hold. Family status was not the final word about opportunity, although family relationships were still important in the society.

These beliefs about individual rights and responsibilities became the basic principles of government in the lands that were settled during the seventeenth and eighteenth centuries. The history of white settlement in the United States may be viewed as a story of individuals and small groups who no longer felt they had to remain in the place or social status that their family had held. That motivation spurred the Pilgrims, the pioneers who crossed the mountains, the homesteaders, and the California gold rush.

It is true that for some people hereditary privilege or the lack thereof continued to be binding. As late as 1860 in the United States, the child of a slave was automatically a slave, although that was more a matter of race than family.

Native Americans continue to exhibit ties to family, tribe,

These two Dutch children arriving at Ellis Island in 1906 would have to rely on their own talents rather than the influence of their family.

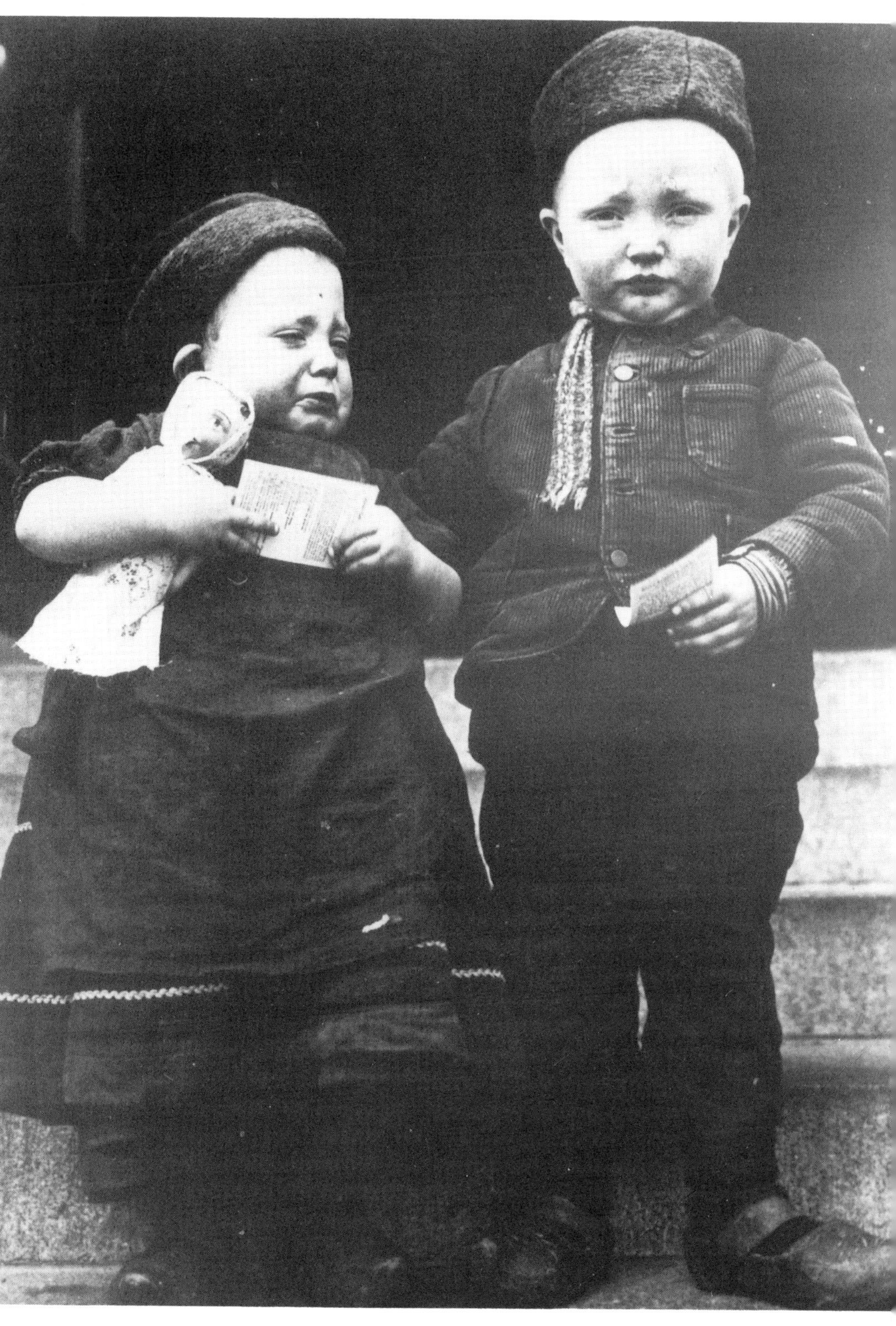

and land that contrast with the more common spirit of individualism. After the great Apache Chief Geronimo had surrendered and was being held at Fort Sill, Oklahoma, he wrote to President Ulysses S. Grant in 1877 asking to return to Arizona. "It is my land, my home, my father's land, to which I now ask to be allowed to return. I want to spend my last days there, and be buried among those mountains." His words clearly express the connection between person, family, and location throughout life.

FAMILY MOLDS

In spite of all the improvement in individual rights and opportunities and the current loose affiliation many people seem to have with their family, there are ways in which a family always influences what a person can accomplish. First of all, the society still has a strong tendency to view a child with the feelings or attitudes that are held about the parents or grandparents.

Think about your first-grade teacher and what that teacher knew about your home and family. No doubt the teacher made certain evaluations of you based on whether or not you were from a single-parent family, the clothes you wore (selected by your parent), the way you ate your food, the words you used. But if the teacher knew your parents more personally, perhaps had even taught one of them in first grade, the connections were stronger.

Being connected to a family can be an advantage if it has a good name or status or talents that are passed on from one generation to another. Thirty percent of the members of the United States Congress had fathers who were politicians. If your mother was a noted artist, it will be easier for you to sell your own paintings (at least the first ones) based on her reputation. In capitalist countries civil law still mandates that personal property be passed on to the next of kin if the will of the deceased does not stipulate otherwise and taxes and debts are paid.

On the other hand family connections can be a disadvantage. If your grandfather served time in prison for robbery, you may come under suspicion in a case of breaking and entering in your neighborhood. If you inherit flat feet or the tendency to be diabetic, you may regret those family ties.

It is not unreasonable for others to evaluate us by our families. After all, we are more like them biologically than like any other human beings, unless we have been adopted. The physical similarities from one generation to another are often striking. If you have the same brown eyes, curly hair, and mouth shape as your father, someone who knows both of you will probably tend to think that you are like him in other ways as well.

The members of your family may tend to have long fingers or short, big feet or small, wide shoulders or narrow, fair skin or dark. Those who have studied genetics know that certain genetic traits are more likely than others to appear from generation to generation. However, the total number of possible traits that may be inherited from your parents alone is staggering. Each human cell normally contains twenty-three pairs of chromosomes, and each gene or combination of genes on the chromosomes controls some aspect of a person's body structure or behavior such as eye color, hair color, height, and intellectual capacity. From the chromosomes in the two cells that combine at your conception, more than seventy trillion combinations of genes are possible. In light of that, it is surprising that any of us resemble our family at all. You could say that your heredity is really just an enormous potential passed on to you from the family gene pool.

Beyond the physical traits we inherit from our parents, we also inherit certain behaviors and intellectual abilities. These are the areas where biologists and psychologists have difficulty determining how much of who we are is the result of heredity and how much is the result of environment. Most of us are cared for as infants by the two people who gave us birth. We get a sort of double-dose input from them, which makes it difficult to say what was inherited and what was learned from experience.

Scientists often study identical twins in an effort to determine how important genetics is in human behavior and appearance. One famous case was the study of Jim Springer and Jim Lewis, identical twins who were separated in infancy and had no contact until they were thirty-nine years old. They not only looked very much alike at that point, but they had similar interests, mannerisms, levels of intelligence, and medical histories. They seemed to have inherited much more than identical physical traits.

The evidence is not so clear when we look at the single child. For example, a woman has great ability as a softball player: She has a good physique for running fast; her reaction time and eye-hand coordination are excellent so she catches and throws well. She was a star player in school and continues to play on her company's team in the city league. From the time her son is a toddler, she plays ball with him. She has him participate in T-ball and buys him good equipment. By the time he is in junior high school he has become a good ball player. The coaches comment on his speed and eye-hand coordination. But who can say how much of his ability is inherited from his mother and how much is due to her encouragement and his early training? All the signs point to the boy's achieving excellence as a ball player, and the role of the mother has certainly been important, but no one can prove exactly how.

THE HAND THAT ROCKS THE CRADLE

Psychologists have established without a doubt that those who care for us in early childhood, usually our parents, have a great effect on our behavior and what we think of ourselves. Our first experiences in the world are with them. In the most basic ways our parents teach us who we are, either positively or negatively. The mother who holds her baby close and sings a lullaby teaches the baby that he or she is precious (an excellent child!), unlike the mother who lets her baby lie in the crib and cry himself to sleep. From the time before our memories develop, we are learning the kind of behavior it takes to achieve what we need or want.

Even if we were not biologically related to those who took care of us in the early years, they would be very important because children learn by modeling the behavior of adults.

Toy manufacturers create miniature lawn mowers, kitchen appliances, and even computers because they know children love to play at what they see adults doing.

This way of learning how to behave and work is most common in the early childhood and preteen years. Then during the teen and young adult years we usually try to do things differently from our parents. We have learned by that time that parents are not perfect, although we may still look and move and behave very much like them.

Most parents are pleased when their children look and act like them. A seven-year-old boy asks for a tie "just like Dad wears," and Dad is proud as he teaches his son how to put on a tie. In similar ways parents like having their children become like them, and they may begin to think that the children will not only follow the same path in life but accomplish things the parent wanted but could not achieve. However, the seventeen-year-old rarely wants anything "just like Dad," and Dad is left wondering why his son has pulled away from him.

When a child grows up to share the parents' interest, has the same aptitudes, or has learned the family skill or occupation, it is not a bad thing for the child to do what the parent has done. The American Revolutionary patriot Paul Revere learned to work gold and silver in his father's smithy and became the leading silversmith of New England. He also tried other related skills such as designing, engraving, bell founding, and dentistry. We remember him chiefly because of the poem written by H. W. Longfellow about his midnight ride on April 18, 1775, to warn the colonists that the British were coming. However, he was captured by the British on that ride and had a very undistinguished career as a soldier. The colonists in and around Boston probably knew him better for his skill in metal working, which he had learned and perhaps inherited from his father.

Many family businesses are passed from parent to child, often for three generations. The Rockefellers in oil and more recently politics, the Barrymores in the theater, the Wyeths in painting, the Menningers in medicine—all these families have made their mark in a particular field because of unusual ability and endeavor by several generations of the family.

A FAMILY OF EXCELLENCE

Does one's family have anything to do with being a person of excellence? A simple answer is yes, it does matter to some extent because of what you inherit and learn from your family. If excellence means high achievement in a particular area combined with high levels of moral behavior, you may want to evaluate your family with those points in mind. Most of us can look at our families somewhat objectively by the time we are teenagers. Analyze the members of your family by asking the following questions:

- What are they good at doing?
- Have several members of your family done one kind of work or hobby or sport?
- Are you like one parent or the other? In what ways?
- Name something you do that pleases your parents. Why?
- Do your parents tell you what jobs or goals you should have?
- Does any kind of disease or handicap affect your family?
- How do members of your family react when crises or disappointments happen?
- How does your family help you perform at the highest level of what you want to be?

In assessing your family, don't forget the qualities of love and trust for one another and encouragement and help when they are needed. Are the members of your family honest with one another? Do they respect the rights of other people? You may not have thought of these attitudes as family benefits, but they are more important than anything else in helping us achieve excellence. When Dad gets drunk and beats Mom on a regular basis, it doesn't make much difference whether he has

This three-year-old boy is full of admiration for his father and wants to be just like him when he grows up.

money or not. The family is still poor, and the child's chances of achieving are lowered.

To reverse the situation, we can see many families that had little or no means of income but gave their children a sense of worth and concern for others that served as a foundation for great achievement. Mother Teresa's father died when she was a small girl in Yugoslavia, leaving the family in dire circumstances, but her mother never stopped sending the children with food to the poor or inviting those who had nothing to share meals with the family. After Teresa became a nun she could not put aside the inspiration of her mother's words and actions. Now the Sisters of Charity work all over the world for the poor, the sick, and the abused, and Mother Teresa has received many awards including the Nobel Prize for her efforts.

A CHILD OF EXCELLENCE

Beyond all the evidence of our family's influence and importance in what we become, points must be made on the other side:

1. No two people are ever exactly alike. Regardless of how much we may inherit from a parent in biological, intellectual, or behavioral likeness, we will not be exactly like either parent. The fingerprint is a simple example. Your genetic potential for excellence is unique.
2. No person ever lives in the same timeframe as his or her parents. Time marches on, things change. The child in school thirty years ago used books, the chalkboard, and the globe to learn. Today a child is more likely to use a computer and video. Relationships with students from other races and cultures are much more possible now, but the study of history is less prevalent. All these changes have an effect on how a person is equipped

Mother Teresa was awarded the Nobel Prize for her tireless work among the poor in India.

to achieve excellence beyond what the family may provide.

3. Finally, no person can escape responsibility for his or her own life. We are to a great extent free to make our choices and to seek our way in life, but with that freedom comes responsibility. If your family is wealthy, you may have many opportunities for education and travel and specialized training, but if you do not make an effort to use those advantages, the wealth won't help you achieve your goals.

   If your family is low- to middle-income like most families, you may feel you don't have any opportunities. That is rarely true. You may have to work harder than others, but no one can stop you from seeking to develop whatever abilities you have or from treating others honestly and fairly. The choices are yours. Life is more a matter of playing the cards you continue to draw from the deck than of having to play only one hand.

Since the 1940s three generations of one family have dominated the NASCAR circuits in the United States. The grandfather, Lee Petty, started racing stock cars as a means of earning extra income for his family of four. He was a tough competitor, and by 1954 he had earned the NASCAR championship. During those years his son, Richard, was helping him work on the race car (a 1949 Plymouth) in the garage at home and going out on the circuits in the summers.

When Richard was twenty-one he began to race on his own with his father's encouragement. He says he never thought of doing anything else. He won seven NASCAR championships, and along the way he introduced his son, Kyle, to the sport. In 1979, Kyle began to race on the circuit.

Seeing the three men together, you notice the same lanky but relaxed athletic build. Richard and Kyle have the same nose and mouth shape. All are known for being fierce drivers on the track, although Lee has not raced since 1961. And each son has been intent on racing better than his father. Each generation has been challenged and taught by the preceding one to strive for excellence in this dangerous sport, but neither

Richard Petty and his son Kyle share a passion for stock car racing.

father put pressure on his son to become a race driver.

We can summarize what we have been saying here. Your mom and dad do make a difference because of the traits and characteristics you inherit from them and because of what they teach you about how to act in the world around you. But they don't control what you do with what you have inherited or been taught. They don't control what others think of you or how you treat other people. Excellence is your own baby! Aren't you glad!

CHAPTER 6

Winning and Excellence: The Same or Different?

People probably pay more attention to sports than any other topic except the weather. We participate in sports on the court, on the floor, or on the field; we attend sporting events as spectators; we watch sports on television; we read the sports sections of the newspapers. Almost everyone has a favorite sporting activity and memories of special sports events.

Many of us were watching the final round of diving competition in the 1988 Summer Olympics when Greg Louganis became the first man to win gold medals in both the diving events that he had won in the 1984 Games—springboard and platform diving. His grace and precision were stunning, especially in light of having hit his head during the springboard preliminaries. In the gymnastics competitions of the 1984 Olympics, Mary Lou Retton thrilled viewers with her performances on the uneven parallel bars, in the vault and exciting

Greg Louganis demonstrates his outstanding abilities during the platform diving event at the Seoul Olympics.

floor routine. She was named best all-around Olympic gymnast. The judges awarded these outstanding competitors the highest ratings for their excellent performances. They were clearly winners.

Achieving excellence requires knowing the standards for performance in the area of your interest, knowing your own talents, working to develop them, and treating others with integrity and respect. Let us look more specifically at how we achieve goals and how that ties in with being a person of excellence. What does it mean to be a winner?

WINNING WAYS AND REWARDS

Winning is a very big thing for most of us. In the early years of school we are urged to work for the gold star. We learn the value of blue ribbons, trophies, inscribed bronze plaques, coming in first, being at the top of the list. "Winning isn't everything; it's the only thing" is a familiar saying, although there is some question whether Vince Lombardi really said it or not. In many ways we learn that competing to be a winner is the right approach no matter what we're doing.

Putting that high value on winning is reinforced by living in a capitalistic society. When an economy regulates itself in a competitive market by the laws of supply and demand, the businesses and persons who make the most money are the ones that compete best. They learn what customers want and how to supply it in the most cost-effective way. They constantly try to stay ahead of competitors who provide the same product. That's what free enterprise is all about.

Competing in order to "win" is also a natural result of strong emphasis on individual rights in the laws and court decisions of a country. When all persons are guaranteed equal opportunity by law, the principal way any person can achieve status is by performing better than another, that is, being a winner, so long as his or her efforts do not violate the rights of others. That kind of legal basis for government makes its citizens put high value on being a "rugged individual" or a "self-made man."

A good deal of our thinking about competition and winning

in the last hundred years has come from the scientific areas of biology and natural history as a result of the work of the British naturalist Charles Darwin. Beginning with his five-year cruise on the *Beagle*, Darwin investigated many natural forms and species of life. In 1859 he published his conclusions in his famous book, *On the Origin of Species*. Darwin believed that plant and animal species struggle for survival and that the ones that do survive and reproduce have developed variations that are best suited to their environment. The term "survival of the fittest" originated with Darwin's theory and was originally only a biological term. Now we hear it applied to many areas of competition.

So our business practices, our governmental structure, and scientific theory all support the notion of competing to win. However, it may be most clearly seen in sports activities. Sports are engaged in at several levels, and the way we compete differs according to the level. At the simplest level are games played for fun and exercise. Each summer Saturday afternoon a group of teenage boys in my neighborhood gather to play baseball. The teams rarely have the same members from week to week. Even the position of home plate may change depending on the time of day and angle of light. It's not serious competition, but they must be having a lot of fun: They keep playing week after week.

The greatest number of sports activities are at the amateur level, most of them associated with school and university programs. Such sports are becoming more and more serious, with strong emphasis on physical conditioning, long practice periods, and highly organized competition until a "final winner" is selected. The increased competitive pressure in sports is evident in Little League games, in the growing use of steroids among teen athletes, and in the violations of NCAA recruiting rules at the college level. As the competition becomes rougher, the sport is less and less like a game, whether it is volleyball or boxing.

Professional sports are of course the most complex level, where athletes compete as their full-time occupation. When athletes are paid more for this "work" than the President of the United States, we get an idea of how important competitive events are to people who watch. Identifying with a winner in a favorite sport or being able to pick a winner gives the spectator some reward. He has the sense of being a winner himself. This interest in competitive sports can't be called play, and it rarely involves physical exercise beyond going from the car to the stadium or turning on the television, but the search for winners means a lot to people.

Sports competition is structured for either individuals or teams. In the examples of diving and gymnastics at the Olympics, the highest level of amateur sports, we cited two athletes who competed in individual sports. Their performances were evaluated by judges. Other individual athletes competed for the same prize—and some came very close, like the Chinese platform diver Xiong Ni who challenged Louganis. But the basic goal of each competitor was to reach his or her own best level of performance.

We see another kind of individual competition in a martial sport such as karate. Athletes at a certain level of ability, identified by the color of the belt they wear, try literally to beat their opponent. Their movements involve striking with the hands, elbows, knees, and feet, and the blows are aimed at sensitive body parts such as the throat and temples. The movements must follow prescribed forms, but the winner is the one who conquers the other. To win in this kind of sport requires working against an opponent until one person loses. Karate is useful in self-defense and it is definitely a physical activity, but it is a very different kind of competition.

Team sports demonstrate another type of competition. Each of the nine players on a baseball team has a position to play and certain functions to perform if the team is to win. All players must know how to coordinate their actions as a team and how to follow the directions of the coaches and manager. Team sports are particularly interesting to watch because the greater number of competitors increases the kinds of action that can take place. Members of a team share the work of competing against the other team, and they share the success of winning. Television views of the excitement in the locker room show us how a winning team feels.

Think back over your own experiences in competing in the classroom, in sports, or in extracurricular activities and ask yourself several questions:

In martial sports the competition between two people is more direct. One person aims to overwhelm the other.

- What kinds of competitive activities have you done?
- Do you prefer individual or team competition?
- If an individual activity, does it make you work to improve yourself against high standards, or does it pit you against another person?
- Do you like competitive activities that call for using your mind more than your body, or vice versa?
- Which part of competitive activity do you like best—the preparation, the performance, or the reward for winning?
- How long have you been doing your favorite competitive activity?
- Has competition improved your abilities?

- What kind of award do you get for winning? How many awards have you won?

Many of us compete because we want the award. We expect winners to get some kind of award, and the awards can be as different as the kinds of competition. We have already mentioned several awards—medals, prizes, cash awards, and plaques.

Not only do the types of awards differ, but awards are given in different ways as well. In some contests it is clearly winner-take-all. There is only *one* World Series champion. Other rewards are distributed according to the level of accomplishment. The winner of the art show receives a blue ribbon; the second place contestant, a red ribbon; the third place, a white. Finally, some awards are distributed equally to all contestants. Every player on the winning Super Bowl pro football team receives an equal cut of the prize money. Watch several television game shows to see what kind of awards are given and how they are distributed. Can you tell what award each contestant really wants?

COMPETITION AND EXCELLENCE

One of the main reasons we set up awards for winners in competitive activities is the assumption that competition improves performance. Competition is believed to be the strongest motivator for achievement. If that is the case, it is important to be a good competitor in order to achieve excellence.

We think we thrive on competition. Studies show that competition does help individuals improve their speed in certain physical and mental activities. Being part of a competitive team promotes learning among team members, whether it is a research project or a soccer team. Winning a competition seems to bring several rewards. A winner gains recognition, receives an award, and has the thrill of accomplishment. The winner's self-esteem is usually boosted for the moment.

However, author Alfie Kohn writes in *No Contest: The Case Against Competition* that we may actually lose out in our race to win by beating others. To view life as a series of contests rarely helps a person develop the character and outlook required for excellence. Being very competitive does not equal having an inner sense of self-worth.

In fact, winning increases anxiety and the pressure to win again. Mark Spitz set twenty-six world records in his six-year career as a competitive swimmer. In the 1972 Olympics alone, he won seven gold medals. Yet after that event Kohn quotes him as saying, "I became sick of myself. I never knew how far down someone could drop, especially after being up so high."

Most winners in competition do experience a letdown. Someone else wins the next event, or the rules change, or the athlete is injured in practice. After a taste of winning and the attention it brings, a person who no longer wins feels a sense of failure and isolation. The competitive spirit expressed in, "Every man for himself" soon turns out to be, "Every man *by* himself." Nonetheless a competitor hooked on being a winner will compete again and again, thinking it is the cure for feeling so low. That pattern is noticeable among boxers who can't or won't quit the ring long after the time when they should for the sake of their bodies.

Competition can actually hamper motivation and performance in certain areas. People in the creative arts often have personalities that are not suited for competing. Performing well in competition requires that some energy be directed toward beating others rather than on painting the picture, playing the instrument, writing the poem, or casting the bronze. Competition may also not be effective in creative areas because the standards for "winning" are so subjective. A winner may be selected according to the judges' tastes or trends at the time rather than creativity of expression, and thus the desire to create is lowered.

Other kinds of activities seem to suffer in quality when they are set up as competitions. The ability to communicate well on camera or being especially photogenic may tilt a campaign toward a candidate who has little ability or experience in solving problems in government. Newspaper reporters compete to "scoop" the rest by covering an event and getting it in print first. The winner is the fastest, but the story may not be accurate or complete, much less well written.

VOLVO
adidas

Framing activities in the form of a contest also seems to detract from seeing the truth of a situation. The emphasis in debate is on making the strongest argument, not on arguing personal convictions or moral rightness. Style and speed count more than integrity. In the courtroom attorneys argue for their sides of a case in much the same way. The goal is to win for the client within the limits of the law and what the judge will allow, but the truth may not come out.

RUNNING YOUR OWN RACE

If competing against others does not help us improve our performance or self-esteen or to develop integrity, how does a person achieve excellence? After all, excellence means being outstanding or above the rest. To answer that question we shall look at the peculiar balance between thinking well of ourselves and thinking well of others.

The most important aspect of striving toward excellence is having a basic sense of self-worth. If you know you have value and special qualities as a person, you don't have to prove yourself by beating others. In fact, you may do better if you stay away from certain kinds of competition. You do not have to worry about being labeled a failure or to concentrate on the talents of others when yours are just as good or different. Doing well is different from doing better than others.

Comparing cooperative activities and environments, the results are different. The author Scott Peck wrote about his feelings and change in school performance after he left a private boys' school in New England that encouraged rugged individualism and a pecking order of "ins" and "outs." As a high school junior Peck attended a small Quaker school in New York City. There he found a community that promoted his development in every way. There were many differences among the students in appearance, ability, and family back-

Stefan Edberg shows his delight at winning the Wimbledon Tennis Championship by kissing the famous trophy.

ground, but there were no cliques or outcasts. Students were not expected to outdo one another or to fit any special mold. "Perhaps for the first time in my life I was utterly free to be me," wrote Peck in *The Different Drum*. In the more cooperative setting he was able to learn and achieve what had seemed impossible in the former school.

A principle of physics is that the whole is greater than the sum of its parts. The same appears to be true of human efforts. A group is greater than the sum of its individual parts. Efforts can be coordinated and labor divided to achieve efficiency. That is the basic rule of the factory or the construction team. But even in areas that require independent effort such as the creative arts or research science, you can perform much better if you know that you are accountable to another person or that you have the support of a larger group. All of us need to know that we have something to contribute as single units, but we also need to know that we are part of a larger whole.

Here are some choices to consider:

I would like to:

a. make a lot of money.
b. work hard at a job.
c. be part of a team.
d. have a happy family.
e. be my own boss.
f. avoid failure.
g. enjoy what I do.
h. get ahead of others in the same field.
i. have all the answers.

Maybe you would like to check all the choices. At one time or another most of us would. However, life doesn't work that way. No one person ever has all the answers; no one can be his or her own boss completely; most people do not find that making a lot of money also brings them a happy family. Choices have to be made, and they usually involve thinking about yourself and others.

The people who achieve excellence have learned how to make those choices so that the end result is good for all. They know how to set goals and stick to high standards without putting others down. They concentrate on developing their own talents, but they look for ways to work with others when it seems appropriate. Awards and prizes have an extra meaning for them.

Their attitude is like that of the girl with a birthday on December 25 who said, "Everyone gets a present on my birthday." Or like Mayor Andrew Young of Atlanta when someone congratulated him on the city's selection as the site of the 1996 Olympics: "I like being part of a good team. This was a good team."

CHAPTER 7

Pacesetters of Excellence

In every age the importance of excellence is made clear because certain individuals continue to demonstrate excellence by the way they live their lives. A man or woman demonstrates a passion for high personal achievement, integrity, and respect for others in such a way that he or she becomes a pacesetter of excellence. He or she defines the term. This high level of ability and character is usually evident within the person's lifetime, but the full contribution may not be recognized until later. In fact, one of the criteria for excellence is that a person's qualities do not diminish or become tarnished as time goes by.

The records of history, literature, and the current news media are filled with life stories about excellence. We shall look at several people, some real and some fictional, some famous and some not well known, who are clearly pacesetters of excellence. Each of these life stories defines excellence in a unique way

ARISTOTLE, TEACHER OF KINGS

Since the days of ancient Greece the name Aristotle has called to mind great achievement in both science and philosophy. Aristotle was born in 384 B.C. in a small town in northern

Greece. His father was a physician who served the king of nearby Macedonia. Thus as a boy Aristotle became acquainted with the kingdom where he would later tutor Alexander the Great as a teenager. The medical profession was hereditary, and Aristotle's father began teaching him at an early age to observe and analyze many areas of life in order to be a good physician. The boy learned to dissect plants and animals and even assisted in caring for patients. He also was trained by the best teachers in poetry, writing, public speaking, gymnastics, music, and dancing.

Life was promising for Aristotle until both his parents died of disease and he became the ward of a relative. At age eighteen he was sent to Athens to study at the renowned academy of Plato. The new student loved both the academy and the city. He stayed for nineteen years, broadening his study from preparation to be a physician to being a scientist and philosopher. He had found a new home in the environment of the academy, first as student and then as teacher.

Following Plato's death, Aristotle went to a coastal town in Asia Minor at the invitation of the ruler Hermias and stayed for about three years. During that time he did extensive study of marine life, gathered students about him whom he began to teach, and married the ruler's adopted daughter, Pythias. It was a happy marriage, and they soon had a daughter. But once again death interrupted Aristotle's situation. The Persians abducted and tortured Hermias, leaving the area politically unsettled, and Aristotle grieved.

It was good timing when King Philip of Macedonia sent for him to tutor young Alexander. Together Aristotle and Alexander studied Greek literature, medicine, and biology. Much of this instruction took place as teacher and student walked along shady paths or sat on stone benches in a garden. Aristotle later became noted for this style of teaching, which was probably based on the method he had learned from his own father—observing and analyzing as one moved through life.

In 336 B.C., King Philip was assassinated and Alexander had to step into his father's role to lead an expedition against the Persians. Aristotle lost his pupil. At age forty-nine he returned to Athens and established the Lyceum, his own school, where he continued his research and writing. By that time Aristotle had developed the principles of keen observation and common sense that opened up remarkable new areas of knowledge for all those who studied under him. For example, he made it a practice to talk with farmers and fishermen when he was investigating plants and sea animals.

Without microscope or telescope (or even eyeglasses), Aristotle studied a range of topics from how the embryo of a chick develops to how the heavenly bodies move in the sky. He developed a checklist and classification system for plant and animal life, moving from change and movement in nature to a science of things that never change or basic principles of reality and knowledge. In the areas of ethics and politics, Aristotle believed that moral virtue comes from avoiding extreme behaviors of any kind. Thus the generous person is neither stingy nor wasteful. A person is truly happy when fulfilling the function of thinking things through or reasoning—the one thing that human beings can do best.

Once more death forced change in Aristotle's life. When Alexander died of malaria in 323 B.C., the Athenians accused Aristotle of lack of reverence for the gods, probably because of his friendship with Alexander. The teacher fled Athens to the city of Chalcis, where he himself died a year later.

Aristotle's life was punctuated by death and loss—his parents, his great teacher Plato who called him "the reader," his father-in-law Hermias, his benefactor King Philip, his beloved wife Pythias, and finally his outstanding pupil Alexander. However, he seems never to have lost his curiosity about the world or his joy in studying it with others. "God and nature do nothing in vain," he wrote. His objective approach formed the base of modern scientific thought. The gifts of this one man are still an important part of knowledge some 2,500 years later.

On the subject of excellence, Aristotle wrote in a book on ethics which he named for his father, "With regard to excellence, it is not enough to know, but we must try to have and use it."

ANNA PAVLOVA, THE SWAN OF BALLET

Some persons who are recognized for achieving excellence seem to have been possessed with striving for high achievement from a very early age. That is the case with the great Russian ballerina Anna Pavlova. Anna was only eight when her mother took her to see Tchaikovsky's ballet "The Sleeping Beauty" in her home city of St. Petersburg (now Leningrad). The young girl was entranced by the fairyland world of the dancers, and from that night in 1882 she determined to become a ballerina. She waited two years until she was ten and then endured the strenuous selection process for admission to the Imperial Ballet School.

For those who had talent and devoted themselves to the rigorous discipline of the school, it was the best of places and times to study ballet. The royal family of Russia supported two schools for ballet students. Those who were admitted lived in dormitories and received room and board and training free, plus a small stipend. Upon graduation, they received a guaranteed income as members of the corps de ballet for one of the theaters and an opportunity for greater wealth if they achieved solo status. Many of the great names in ballet—Nijinsky, Diaghilev, Fokine—were studying or teaching in Russia at that point. For Anna to have that opportunity must have meant much to her mother, who struggled to support them after the death of her husband.

For seven years Anna studied and kept the vision of being a great prima ballerina. She was not particularly strong and took cod liver oil daily. Her feet were considered ill-shaped for ballet, but no one questioned her determination or her ability to express emotion with her body, hands, and face.

A few nights after her graduation in 1899, she made her debut at the Marinsky Theatre in St. Petersburg, a step that usually took several years to achieve. From struggling student, Anna suddenly was earning seven hundred fifty rubles a year. She and her mother were able to rent a nice apartment, and a carriage waited to drive her to the theater each night. The change in Anna's status at such an early point did not affect her desire to achieve perfection in dance. She continued to practice three hours or more each day and to seek new roles or music to perform.

In 1905 Anna was a leader in instigating strikes against the government for greater artistic freedom for dancers. The first signs of revolt against the Czar were taking place, and

Anna witnessed riots in the streets followed by an outbreak of plague. Nothing stopped her from practicing or performing and attending the performances of her friends.

During this period she married a longtime admirer, Victor Dandre. His quiet strength and calm advice were very important to Anna. At about the same time her friend, Michel Fokine, the choreographer, composed a three-minute solo for her entitled "The Dying Swan," which became the dance she was known for all over the world.

Although people connected with ballet in Russia assumed that Anna would be named *ballerina assoluta*, still Anna worked for perfection. She employed an Italian ballet master named Cecchetti to work with her to overcome some technical flaws. She had performed in Moscow as well as St. Petersburg, but following a brief tour of several European cities in 1908 Anna wanted to dance for people all over the world. She later referred to her first performance outside Russia, in Stockholm, as the turning point in her life.

By the end of 1910 Pavlova had visited every great city of Europe and had made one brief trip to New York. Everywhere her performances were sold out and the theaters mobbed. Royalty entertained her. The king of Spain sent a basket of orchids after seeing her dance for the first time. Anna became a regular performer in London, and she and her husband bought a home in nearby Hampstead. Ivy House became the quiet retreat to which Anna returned after each strenuous tour. She built a studio on the grounds and installed a lake where she kept a pair of swans.

As World War I approached, Anna was detained in Germany during a tour, so she began to tour more in the United States. The American press paid her great attention, and she had a strong influence on style and fashion. Her friends included the silent picture stars Mary Pickford and Charlie Chaplin, and Anna played a starring role in the movie "The Dumb Girl of Portici." But as a result of the strain of work, financial problems

This dancer is following in Anna Pavlova's footsteps. She is dedicating her life to sharing the beauty of classical ballet with people all over the world, rich and poor alike.

related to her touring group, and worry about her mother, who remained in Russia during the war, Anna began having health problems.

For five years Anna traveled wherever tours could be arranged. Sometimes the group traveled by cattle boat and played to barefoot, poverty-stricken audiences. The situation improved when the war ended, but as Anna grew older she seemed to push herself and other dancers harder. She rarely slept more than five hours a night, and she personally inspected each dancer in the troupe before every performance. In South Africa she herself composed a ballet based on the gift of a feather fan.

Pavlova was demanding, but she was never a snob. She would talk to anyone she met on trains, in stations, on the street. She developed an interest in children who were war orphans. She founded a home for them in Paris and performed benefits to support them. Wise enough not to return to Russia, she helped other Russian dancers who managed to leave.

At forty-six Pavlova was still dancing and touring. In the next few years a terrible pain developed in her knee; then in Dublin a piece of scenery fell on her. On doctor's orders she rested for five weeks, but she refused to cancel the opening of a new tour in the Netherlands. On the way there she contracted pleurisy. The doctors recommended a life-saving surgery but one that would prevent her ever dancing again. Anna refused. She could not think of living without dancing. After an illness of six days, she died with her costume for "The Swan" in her hands.

As long as people study ballet, Anna Pavlova will be remembered for her excellence in classical technique. She never lost her passion for her work or her vision of bringing the joy of ballet to people all over the world. She was a pacesetter.

ATTICUS FINCH, MAN OF LAW AND MERCY

The writers of fiction give us heroes and heroines with many different personalities. As readers we are often able to understand a character better than the other characters in the story understand him or her. We know what is going on inside the person or behind the scenes. In that way we are able to recognize the traits of excellence even though the character is not admired by others in the story.

In the novel *To Kill a Mockingbird* by Harper Lee, the attorney Atticus Finch is related to nearly everyone in a small Alabama town; yet he displays intelligence, compassion, and understanding that are beyond the rest. The plot centers around Atticus's defense of Tom Robinson, a black man charged with raping a poor young white woman. At the trial Atticus asks a series of probing, courteous questions, first of the girl's father and then of her. The truth is revealed—it was the father who abused her, not Tom Robinson, whose one arm was so much shorter than the other that he could not possibly have done the actions described by the lying plantiff.

Nonetheless, a white jury votes the black man quilty. As Atticus leaves the courtroom, all the blacks in the balcony stand to honor him. The next morning the back steps of his home are full of gifts of food, the most precious commodity in the South during the Depression.

The girl's father, Bob Ewell, does not feel so kindly toward Atticus. Even after Tom Robinson is killed trying to escape, Ewell knows that Atticus has shown him to be a shiftless liar, and he vows to get even. His attack on the attorney's children is foiled by their friend and neighber, the retarded Boo Radley, who stabs Ewell.

In the character of Atticus Finch, we see a man who comprehends human weaknesses and reveals them in the pursuit of justice. However, what really raises Atticus to a level of excellence is his lack of personal condemnation of others, even though they may be guilty before the law. He has a higher view of equality and compassion. His qualities are recognized by all levels of society and admired by all but the ignorant and evil. At the close of the book, when he is tucking his young daughter in bed, he makes a comment that sums up his philosophy of life: "Most people are [nice], Scout, when you get to know them."

ANGIE AND REAL LIFE AT SEVENTEEN

The examples of excellence that make the greatest impression on us are often those of people who are about our age or in our situation. For many years the writers of fiction did not present real-life situations from the perspective of teens. Novels such as *Huckleberry finn* and *Little Women* use a teenager's viewpoint and have important themes, but they were not written with a teenage audience in mind.

In the early 1940s as the United States was entering World War II, Maureen Daly wrote what is considered one of the first young adult novels. *Seventeenth Summer* portrayed a realistic view of what it was like to be a seventeen-year-old girl at that time. Although the story seems a little out of date now, it still captures the struggle that many teens face in their first romances.

Angie has just graduated from a girls' school when she meets Jack, who delivers for a bakery in the small Wisconsin town where she lives. During the summer their romance develops, and Angie faces the usual doubts and temptations that come with first love. She is afraid that her family may disgrace her when Jack comes for their first date; then she is afraid that he may not measure up to her family's standards.

As she moves in the different circles of dating couples, she goes to beer parties and blanket parties and faces what it means to date a boy with a bad reputation. The major shock is learning that her much-admired older sister has a poor reputation among boys. At the end of the summer Angie and Jack say good-bye, vowing to love each other always, but she knows that their relationship will not stand the separation and that her life will move on because she has different values and goals.

This book was so popular with teenage girl readers in the years after its release that librarians could not keep it on the shelves. One library stocked seventy copies. In a time when adults were caught up in the hard realities of war and finances, teens were delighted to read about a heroine who faced the realities of a teenager—looking for security, being ashamed of one's family, being self-conscious in a crowd, being uncertain how to act in a first romance. The book's continuing popularity is surprising because it does not have the neat and happy ending of many romances. Angie was a new kind of heroine who faced all these situations and in the end decided that she would pursue her goals beyond the local crowd. She had more important things to do with her life than to keep a summer romance going and perhaps become a pregnant teenager. She made the choice for broader options and opened the door to excellence.

FLORENCE GRIFFITH-JOYNER, WORLD'S FASTEST WOMAN

Florence Griffith-Joyner is a pacesetter in several ways. She has beaten the odds and the clock. She was the seventh of eleven children. Her parents divorced when she was four, and her mother and the children moved to the Watts section of Los Angeles. Florence started running track when she was seven. She remembers that she always won the 50- and 70-meter dashes in elementary and junior high school.

The Griffiths had strict family rules, with no TV during the week and early bedtime. Once a week they had family "powwows" when they read the Bible and talked about what they had done during the week. Florence, or Dee Dee as the family called her, kept a diary and wrote poetry. Although the family were poor, they didn't seem to know it.

After graduation from high school where she had set school records in sprinting, Florence went to California State University at Northridge, but she had to drop out to work after her freshman year. Her assistant track coach, Bob Kersee, recognized her talent and helped her get financial aid. In 1980 Florence transferred to UCLA to continue training under Kersee. She won NCAA championships in the 200-meter event in 1982 and in the 400 in 1983. She was also establishing her reputation for stylish flair with long fingernails painted in rainbow colors.

When she came in second rather than first in the 1984 Olympic 200-meter event, she pulled back from training and began working at a Los Angeles bank during the day and as a hairdresser at night. In 1987 she resumed serious training with Kersee, with the 1988 Games in view, and she married Al Joyner, a 1984 Olympic gold medalist in the triple jump. When she came in second again in the 200 in the World Games in 1987, she decided that she had a choice: She could either accept that she was second-best, or she could become the best.

She began daily track workouts and weight-training sessions four times a week. She ran almost four miles a day. She began to train for longer races and always thought of herself as winning the 200.

In the United States Olympic track and field trials in July 1988, Florence Joyner ran the four fastest 100 meters in women's track history. In the Summer Olympics in Seoul the following September, she again set new records and earned three gold medals and one silver. FloJo had excelled without question.

Although her coach attributed her amazing performance to her strength and endurance, Florence told a reporter for New York *Newsday*: "It takes experience—time—to get strength, to learn to concentrate on what you have to do . . . confident that nobody else in that race can run with you."

Early in 1989 she announced her retirement to do the writing, designing, and modeling she wants to do, and she continues to coach her husband. She has received many honors from all over the world, including the 1988 Sullivan Award as the top American athlete and the Harvard Foundation Award for outstanding contributions to society. It will be interesting to see what pace she sets for excellence in her future endeavors.

PERSONAL PACESETTERS

As we review these pacesetters of excellence (really a very small sample), we notice their personalities and characteristics. They persist in doing the things they believe in; they use their talents, whether physical or mental, to achieve goals; they face difficult situations but continue to seek opportunities for what they want to achieve; and they treat others with respect. They point the way to excellence for all of us.

You probably have your own examples of pacesetters of

Florence Griffith-Joyner celebrates her victory in the 100-meter dash at the 1988 Olympic Games in Seoul.

SEOUL 19
569
mes of the 24th Olympiad
545

excellence. We can nearly always find people around who are good models of what we want to become. One of my heroes is a man named Robert Allen, who recently received his doctorate in English. That doesn't sound so remarkable until you learn that his parents divorced a few months before he was born, and his mother deserted him when he was six years old.

Robert spent his childhood secluded with older relatives, one of whom refused to let him go to school. He sat around listening to stories from past days and to book after book read to him by a great-aunt. He completely missed grade school and high school and was about twelve when he began reading on his own. He started with Shakespeare! He picked up anything he could find: comic books, mythology, poetry, ancient history, anything related to the Bible. He didn't know that kids his age "weren't supposed to be reading those things."

When he was about thirty Allen decided to get his high school diploma. He took the GED even though he was afraid he would not pass. He scored 95! Then he took the College Level Examination Program exam and scored high enough to skip the first year of college. He entered a small church-related college on government-paid tuition at age 32. His clothes were in tatters, and his shoes had holes in them. He had never been to a dentist and had lost his front teeth. But his fellow students soon learned that he was the kindest human being they had ever met, in addition to being very intelligent. He graduated summa cum laude in three years and accepted a fellowship for graduate study.

Today Allen is a poet and teacher. He has no family but many friends. He lives a simple, quiet life with his cat Sparkplug. He drives a 1981 Ford unless he walks. Although people are awed by his intellectual accomplishments and generosity and he has been featured in local and national publications and television shows, Robert Allen remains modest and content to make the most of whatever situation life brings. He looks to the future and enjoys creating poems for today.

Although Robert Allen could be put in the class of celebrity,

In his tenacity and endurance, Nelson Mandela has been an inspiration to many people.

he does not seek the limelight. He could capitalize on what he has accomplished and attain power, money, and more attention. However, he is interested in other values. He lives on the basis of courage and self-discipline, which have greater potential for long-lasting excellence. It is easy to confuse being a celebrity with being a true hero.

Think about the people you admire: perhaps a well-known person like South African Nelson Mandela or actress Carol Burnett or basketball star Michael Jordan; perhaps the woman doing volunteer literacy work in your town or the man leading the campaign to save virgin forests or the bald eagle. Whoever they are, they give you the feeling that you can make it, that you can reach the high ideals we call excellence. They are your pacesetters.

CHAPTER 8

The Quest for Excellence

Any list of famous explorers of the earth's surface has the name of Captain James Cook near the top. This English seaman was remarkable in several ways. In the years 1768 to 1779 he sailed three great voyages around the world. He mapped the coasts of New Zealand and eastern Australia, discovered numerous islands in the Pacific, sailed around Antarctica and proposed that it was a continent, discovered Hawaii, mapped the northwest coast of America, and searched for a passage through the Arctic Ocean.

Other factors, however, set Cook's quest apart from the explorations of such adventurers as Christopher Columbus, Vasco da Gama, and Ferdinand Magellan. Cook's first expedition to the South Seas was commissioned to chart the transit of Venus as a means of determining the earth's distance from the sun. With the help of newly invented instruments, he was one of the first to be able to determine his exact position on the earth at almost any hour of the day or night. His maps were so carefully prepared that returning to the same location was no longer an accident.

The accomplishment of which Cook himself seems to have

been most proud was the conquest of scurvy. Most voyages of the time were ruined or cut short after about three months by this disease, which drained energy, made teeth fall out, and opened old wounds as if they had never healed. Cook did not know about vitamin C, but he knew that vegetables and lemons somehow prevented scurvy, so he loaded his ship with sauerkraut, condensed lemon juice, and a special malt combination. At each port he had sailors collect and eat as much fresh green food as possible. He changed the systems of watches on board so that men had longer to rest and dry out their clothes. He insisted that quarters and clothes be kept clean. It was much less risky to be a sailor on board one of Cook's ships.

In his efforts to improve scientific knowledge and to maintain the health of seamen, and in his treatment of the native peoples he encountered on his voyages, Cook advanced the interests of his country and mankind as a whole. The names of the ships he commanded on his three voyages suggest his spirit: *Endeavor, Resolution,* and *Adventure*.

Such an effort to discover and pursue new ideas and experiences is often referred to as a quest. The word *quest* began to be used by the French in the Middle Ages, usually to refer to some noble expedition by a knight such as the quest for the Holy Grail, the cup or chalice Jesus used at the Last Supper. The word was also used to refer to the search for game by hounds because of the sense of pursuit and determination it carried.

You will notice that *quest* is much like *question*. Both are from the same Latin root, *querere,* to seek or inquire. To question something is to seek the answer, to look for new information. All quests and questions begin with curiosity, something inside the person who wants to learn. In this chapter we shall look at how this desire to explore contributes to excellence.

In the children's game Twenty Questions, one player thinks of a person, place, or thing and other players try to guess what it is by asking up to twenty questions. Players may answer only by saying "Yes," "No," or "I don't know." If a player can guess correctly before using up twenty questions, he or she becomes "it." If not, the first player gets another turn. The game can be a lot of fun, and it certainly teaches us something about how to ask questions.

The things we learn most easily are usually those that we are curious about, that we really want to know for one reason or another. We can develop or continue a process of asking questions about almost anything. For example, you might be interested in endangered species of animals. That raises a great many questions:

- Which ones are endangered?
- Where do they live?
- Where can they be seen? In zoos? In circuses? In the wild?
- Why are they endangered? Are they used for clothing? For food? For trophies?
- What are the life cycles of these animals? How long will it take to replenish the species?
- What is the government doing to protect such animals?
- Are private groups working in their behalf?

It would not be hard to go well beyond twenty questions on this topic. And such a list can be generated on any topic, from a specific subject such as paper airplanes to a broad topic such as rock music stars. The game Trivial Pursuit is based on questions about peculiar or little-known facts that some people remember.

You may be surprised at the number of things you actually have questions about in the course of a week. Such questions pop into our heads and are gone unless we keep a record of them or something causes us to remember them. Try keeping a list called, "Things I want to know" or "Questions I have" in a notebook or pocket pad. You are probably a lot more curious than you realized.

Questions are significant for your personal development of excellence in several ways. For one thing they point toward your interests. Let your curiosity have free rein for a while, and keep a record of all your questions. Then review the questions and arrange them by subject area or in order of importance to you. If your list has a number of questions about construction or building, you probably have a strong interest or aptitude in engineering. If you have questions about why people do things

The natural curiosity of these kindergarten children leads them to an exploration of geometric forms.

in a certain way, you may want to study sociology. In that way questions can be a starting point for your quest.

Biographies of the great inventor Thomas Alva Edison often begin with his chemistry experiments in the baggage car of the train between Port Huron and Detroit, Michigan, where he sold newspapers and snacks in the late 1850s. But his enormous curiosity was evident much earlier. His mother had been a schoolteacher, and she remembered some of his early questions: "How does a hen hatch chickens?" "Why does water put out a fire?" When he entered school his teacher whipped him for asking so many questions. One day he overheard the schoolmaster tell someone that he was "addled." Edison ran home to tell his mother, and she immediately took him out of school. She believed that learning should be fun, and she began to teach him at home. When he was nine she bought him a chemistry book, and he tested every experiment himself to try to prove the author wrong. From this early beginning and with only three months of formal schooling, Edison went on to invent motion pictures, the telephone transmitter, the stock ticker, the mimeograph machine, the phonograph, and in 1879 the electric light. The end result of Edison's great curiosity has been to reshape everyday life for all of us.

Edison's story illustrates another point about the role of questions: They are only the starting point. Their greatest value lies in motivating us to action—to find the answers or, as in Edison's case, to see if someone else's answers are right. Questions lead us on quests. We have to make the effort for discovery. Edison knew that. He is often quoted as saying, "There is no substitute for hard work."

NEW WRINKLES

As we take up our quests, find answers to our questions, we store the new data in the most amazing organ of creation—the human brain. The average weight of a human brain is three and a half pounds. The number of brain cells is estimated at ten billion. For a long time it was believed that each time a human being learned something, it created a new crease or wrinkle in the tissue of the brain. Thus a person who knew more would have more creases in his or her brain.

Now we know that it is more accurate to say that each time we learn something we create a new electrical connection from one part of the brain tissue to another. These signals depend upon the production of certain chemical substances, especially one called dopamine. When the connection is made, a new code is embedded so that the information or experience is stored for later retrieval and use. Just how that happens is still being studied. We do know that one human brain far exceeds the power of the most massive mainframe computer yet invented.

All sorts of data and memories are stored in the brain. The five senses are the basic receivers for such input, and some of us receive better through one sense or combination of senses than another. The sense of sight is generally considered the most important. We look at pictures, videos, film, real objects, symbols such as words on pages like this, and countless other

images that pass before our eyes each day. All are encoded in the brain tissue. We also receive much through our ears. We hear radios, audio tapes, live broadcasts, the speech of others, the sounds of music, motors, and mayhem. All is encoded. In the same way we benefit from the senses of touch, taste, and smell. Depending on your interests and occupation, these are of varying importance. If you are a violinist, the senses of touch and sound are critical. If you are a chef, the senses of taste and smell are more important.

All the senses contribute to our quest for answers. We seek the resources that we need and collect the data. How much we take in is governed first of all by how receptive we are. You may have played another childhood game called Observation. Someone places ten to twenty objects on a table and covers them with a cloth. The players are called into the room, the cloth is removed, and they have one minute to observe the objects. Then the players have five minutes to write down all they can remember. The person who remembers the most is the winner.

Why people remember what they receive through their senses is a large area of psychological investigation called perception. In Observation one person remembers a cup on the table because it is blue, another because it is just like one she has at home, another because he collects cups, another because of a cup in a story. The connections already made in the brain act to affect the encoding of new data.

A detective once staged an automobile accident between two actors at a busy intersection. Seven witnesses to the accident were asked to describe what they had seen. Of course, no two stories were alike, yet no person was intentionally not telling the truth. The difference was in their perception and the variety of human experience. Some had better vision than others, some were at one angle and some at another, some had been in accidents themselves and others had not, and so on.

Thomas Edison in his laboratory holding the "Edison Effect" bulb, on which all the science of modern electronics is based.

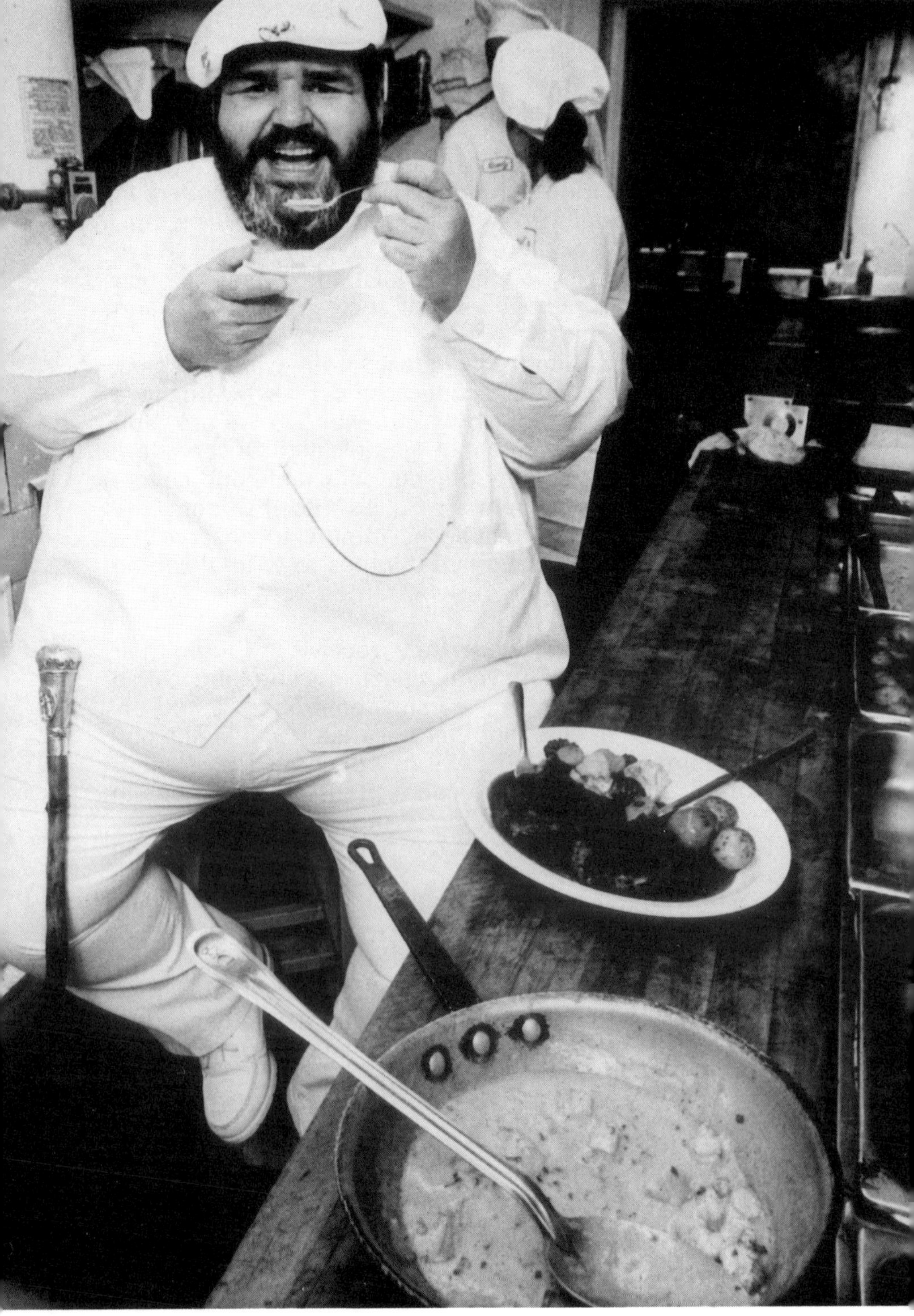

We cannot control all the factors that affect our perception, but we can train ourselves to be more observant, to take more time for receiving and analyzing material that may have the answers we need. That gives the brain a chance to make the connection with what is already stored there, to make a new wrinkle.

The endless bits of information we store in our brain come back to us in two basic ways:

1. Randomly without effort on our part when we daydream, dream in sleep, or are under the influence of drugs.
2. On demand from the conscious mind.

Our random thought patterns are often very interesting, even inspiring. They provide us with sudden insights and exciting breakthroughs in knowledge. However, any quest for achievement relies mainly on the ability to recall previously learned material.

The process of memory is not fully understood, but its significance is illustrated by our referring to the capacity of a computer to store information as "memory." The more capacity or memory a computer has, the more functions it can perform. It is better able to make connections and changes in the material that is received. No one knows how much unused capacity each of us has in our brain—probably about ninety percent!

TREASURES EVERYWHERE

As remarkable as the brain is, we cannot expect it to store everything, nor should it. From the days of the caveman, humans have stored useful information in different forms for future reference and use by others. When things and actions began to be represented by standard written symbols known

Chef Paul Prudhomme relies on his keen sense of taste and smell in perfecting the dishes he creates for his Louisiana Kitchen.

by a large group of people, communication through language took a great leap forward. Over the centuries certain places developed a reputation for their collections of information. Among them was the most famous library of ancient times, at Alexandria, Egypt, which may have contained as many as 700,000 papyrus scrolls.

With the Chinese invention of paper around 105 A.D., the world had a more suitable element for storing information, and the demand for written material could not be satisfied with handwriting. The Koreans developed printing from movable type in the 1300s, and Johannes Gutenberg of Germany began printing books from his invention of movable type in the 1400s. The advent of the printed book opened the door for libraries much as we know them today—shelves of books against walls with tables nearby for reading. Many of the world's great library collections started during the fifteenth and sixteenth centuries, and those collections became hubs for great centers of learning and new advances in knowledge.

These paper pages with words printed on them and bound together in a cover for easy storing and carrying are such a universal part of life that we rarely think about it. Yet books have contained the treasures of all achievement of life on earth. Excellence cannot be achieved without relying on what has been preserved of the work of others in books. People die, but their thoughts are preserved. We can choose our friends, so to speak, from the great people of history. The English poet Joseph Addison understood that as early as 1711 when he wrote:

"Books are the legacies that a great genius leaves to mankind, which are delivered down from generation to generation, as presents to the posterity of those who are yet unborn."

As more knowledge accumulated, more data were available for storage and retrieval. Other forms besides the book were invented for storing information, nearly all of them dependent upon electricity and artificial substances such as plastic. Information is now stored on microfiche, videos, audio tapes, records, and compact discs, not to mention computers.

When computers came into use, the multiplication of knowledge was astounding. Now you can seek answers from many libraries by using the computer network in one library or a

In conjunction with books, computers are an invaluable information source and teaching aid in all schools.

modem connection through your phone at home. We live in an age known for its "information boom." Any person's quest is sure to turn up information. It is no excuse to say that answers cannot be found!

However, we do have to define our questions clearly. (If you want to know how birds fly, don't look up reference sources on penguins.) We also have to practice using the sources. (If the article you need on the origin of buck dancing is on microfiche, you need to know how to operate the fiche reader.) And we have to do some detective work to find which sources are most likely to have the answers we need. (If you want to know more about cannons during the Civil War, don't go to a medical library.)

Perhaps the most exciting part of looking for answers is that they may be found in unexpected places if we have our eyes open. On a recent broadcast of "All Things Considered" on public radio, Ms. A. B. Smith, a fifth-grade teacher in West Point, Mississippi, described the weekly Saturday afternoon trips she and her sister took as children with their father. They would pile into the dilapidated family station wagon and go from trash pile to trash pile along the country roads. At each stop their father called out, "Diamond rings and earbobs waiting to be found." The girls would jump out and search the trash for any usable items, although diamonds were never turned up. But Ms. Smith did find copies of *The Iliad, The Odyssey,* and *The Arabian Nights* in one pile, and from that start she read as much as she could. She believes that her discoveries were much more valuable than diamonds.

Many times the best source of answers is another person who is looking for the same kind of information or who has experience in the same kind of quest. When you ask another person for information, you tap into that person's brain for material to store in yours. This transmission of knowledge from one person to another is still at the root of all sources of information, no matter what kind of material we use. Knowledge is for sharing. That's how treasure is multiplied.

ORIGINAL HOT-WIRING

The wonder of being human is endless. As exciting as it is to experience new sensations through the senses and to find answers to questions that interest us, what set us apart as the highest form of life on the planet are our abilities to imagine and to change both ourselves and our environment. As a result of these human abilities we literally have galaxies in which to live and move and have our being.

The quest for excellence might be described as the processing of data and experiences in order to make changes. We pursue goals in order to find meaning or learn new ways. How do you make changes for reaching your goals? In *Schooling for Individual Excellence,* Don Parker describes the process of change as a spiral that starts at birth and continues over the course of life. A person "learns" something at one level and spends time to incorporate that new behavior or insight into past experience. After a certain period the person is ready to move forward again, powered by the recent learning.

In this theory we move through life from one level to the next in a series of spirals rather than on a smooth incline. Each time a person learns something new, it generates enough power or change to provide motivation for the next loop. And each new loop is larger than the last because it contains all the previous loops.

We can see this process clearly if we think of it as developing a new skill and then applying it. A person learns a new software program and then uses it in writing projects. Later he or she can learn another software program for accounting. However, that program will be easier to learn because of the experience with the first program.

This approach to learning is often purposely built into situations. In the early elementary grades of some school systems, the major skills are taught in the first, third, and fifth grades, with the second and fourth grades concentrating on reinforcement or application of those skills. Training programs at factories are set up so that a new employee learns a set of skills and then practices them before moving on to a higher level of skill.

Another way of thinking about how we change is called the "scientific method." Simply put, that process involves stating the question or problem, collecting information, forming a hypothesis, testing the hypothesis, and reaching a conclusion. If you turn on your tape player and nothing happens, you have a problem. You collect certain information such as whether or not the tape is in place, the right button is turned on, the batteries are good, and so on. As you investigate all these possibilities, you are collecting information, forming theories about the problem, and testing those theories. Based on the results, you will make changes to start your tape player.

In the modern age, the scientific approach has been widely used and promoted as the best basis for making discoveries and gaining knowledge. It does produce results, but it may not work so well in areas that involve complex human behavior. For example, applying the method to the causes of labor

NEW YORK
NEWSPAPER
PRINTING PRESSMEN'S
UNION NO. 2
UNFAIR LABOR
PRACTICE
STRIKE
DAILY NEWS

strikes is complicated because the subject is so broad and because the circumstances from one strike to another are never the same.

The scientific method has become associated with the idea of work or serious effort because of the investigation requirements and sequence of steps to be carried out. We often look for ways to achieve our goals that do not call for work. We want to enjoy what we do, and few people seem to enjoy their "work."

In *The Adventures of Tom Sawyer*, Mark Twain depicted that attitude about work and play in the episode of Tom's whitewashing the fence. Tom did not want to spend his Saturday morning at the job Aunt Polly insisted that he do. When his friend Ben Rogers came along, Tom pretended that painting was a rare opportunity for great fun. In the end Ben was so eager to do the job that he bribed Tom with an apple just to get to paint. By afternoon Tom had not only been able to get others to do his work but he had collected quite a few treasures in exchange for the "privilege."

Twain cleverly demonstrated that the difference between work and play is all in attitude.

In fact, we start life with little distinction between the two. Watch some three-year-olds in a sandbox. They concentrate on the job of moving and building. They are very serious about digging, piling, making roads, filling dump trucks. They are really working at it, but it is always called play. And it *is* play because they are doing it with pleasure. The three-year-olds are having fun making changes in the contours of the sand.

That kind of effort is both spontaneous and highly motivated. We do best what we want to do. We are at our most creative when there is no division between "work" and "play" in our minds. A lot of effort must still be put forth to make the changes required to meet our goals, but it doesn't feel like effort because we sense that something new is being developed. Creativity is not passive. I can watch someone's creative efforts as portrayed on television and have creative ideas as a

It is impossible to understand the complexity of human social behavior by applying a purely scientific method.

result, but no change will occur if I do not take action on the ideas.

The popular author Caroline Cooney has published more than forty books for both adults and teens. She loves to write. When asked where she gets her ideas, she says it's hard to say because " . . . my mind is so filled with ideas that it is more a matter of sifting among them than struggling to come up with one." But success did not come without effort. Ms. Cooney had written ten novels before any of them were sold.

Each of us has a unique rate of intellectual, physical, and emotional growth. Each of us lives in a different environment with different experiences. You are not a name brand. You are an original, and you have something "new" to develop. All things new start with an idea or an inner awareness, some picture in your mind that has power. You then take action on what you have imagined in order to reach a goal. You do research to answer questions; you store the information in your brain and combine it in different ways with the ideas of others. What you create is the unique change you have to share. It is the result of your quest.

Captain Cook went around the world three times. He discovered many islands and two continents. He charted the oceans and helped chart the planets. He made the first reliable maps of the sea, and he conquered scurvy. In one of his journals he wrote that he had a great desire to go "not only farther than any other man has been before me, but as far as I think it possible for man to go." His vision led him to make great changes and provide new information for all the world. It was a unique quest for excellence.

CHAPTER 9

The Difference Excellence Makes

The spirit of excellence can be seen at work in groups as well as in the lives of individuals. We have already discussed some of the many ways one may strive for and achieve excellence. Given the great variety that exists in the talent, opportunity, personal effort, and family background of one person, it is amazing when a group of people can catch the same vision of excellence and work together to attain it. Let us examine some of the major group structures in our culture—businesses, schools, communities, and governments—to see how excellence is achieved within a group.

BUSINESS ORGANIZATIONS

In capitalist countries like the United States, the business organization is the single most important structure in the society. The business that a person works for becomes very significant in his or her life, whether it's a three-person shoe-repair shop or a three thousand-employee auto plant. The place where we earn income to meet our living expenses is a major part of our lives. Many adults spend more waking hours

McDonald's founder Ray Kroc, in front of one of the 7,500 franchises that now exist throughout the world.

at work than they do anywhere else. They may feel closer to the people in the business than to the members of their family. Like it or not, the owners, managers, and employees of a business are all in the same boat. If they want to stay afloat, to stay "in business," they have to work toward certain common goals. How well they do that is the best indicator of their success as a business.

The role of excellence in capitalism or in being a successful business has been much discussed in recent years. American business owners began to pay attention to it as advances in technology changed the way businesses produced goods for sale and managed their operations. The increased competition from other countries also required greater attention to quality. Excellence became more critical.

Two men, Thomas J. Peters and Robert H. Waterman, Jr., studied seventy-five highly regarded American companies in 1979–80 to discover what kind of management makes a company successful over a long period of time. What makes a business strive for excellence?

Their findings are described in their book *In Search of Excellence*. It contains interesting stories about how businesses determined what was important and how they worked toward those goals. For example, each of the McDonald's hamburger outlets is measured in four categories: quality, service, cleanliness, and value. Each employee is drilled in Q,S,C&V (as they are known). The founder and head of McDonald's, Ray Kroc, personally visited and inspected stores to make sure they met those standards. The owners and managers agree that offering the customer consistently high levels in those areas, no matter where the store is located, is their means to a successful business.

Paying attention to customers is an important part of motivating many companies toward high performance and quality. Certainly they want to sell and make a profit on their product or service, but successful companies seem to have their customers' best interests in mind even when an immediate profit is not in the picture. The Maytag Company has a goal of giving "ten years trouble-free operation," and it makes that goal clear in its TV commercials showing the lonely Maytag repairman.

The Johnson & Johnson Company exhibited its concern for customers in 1982 when a few bottles of its pain reliever Tylenol were discovered to have been laced with cyanide. The company already had in place an ironclad ethics policy, which formed the basis for its immediate action when the poisonings were discovered. It recalled millions of dollars worth of the product, sponsored ad campaigns and toll-free hotlines to alert the public and answer questions, and put up reward money to help find those responsible for the crime. The company's previous commitment to "doing the right thing" helped it to handle the situation quickly and emerge with a good reputation.

In addition to treating customers right, the truly successful companies know that treating their employees with respect is important. The Levi Strauss Company is world famous for making blue jeans, a kind of pants originally designed for the hard work of mining and ranching. Jeans, usually Levi's, are almost a national uniform. Following the San Francisco earthquake in 1906, the Levi Strauss Company established itself as a company that cared about its employees though much of its business had been destroyed by the disaster.

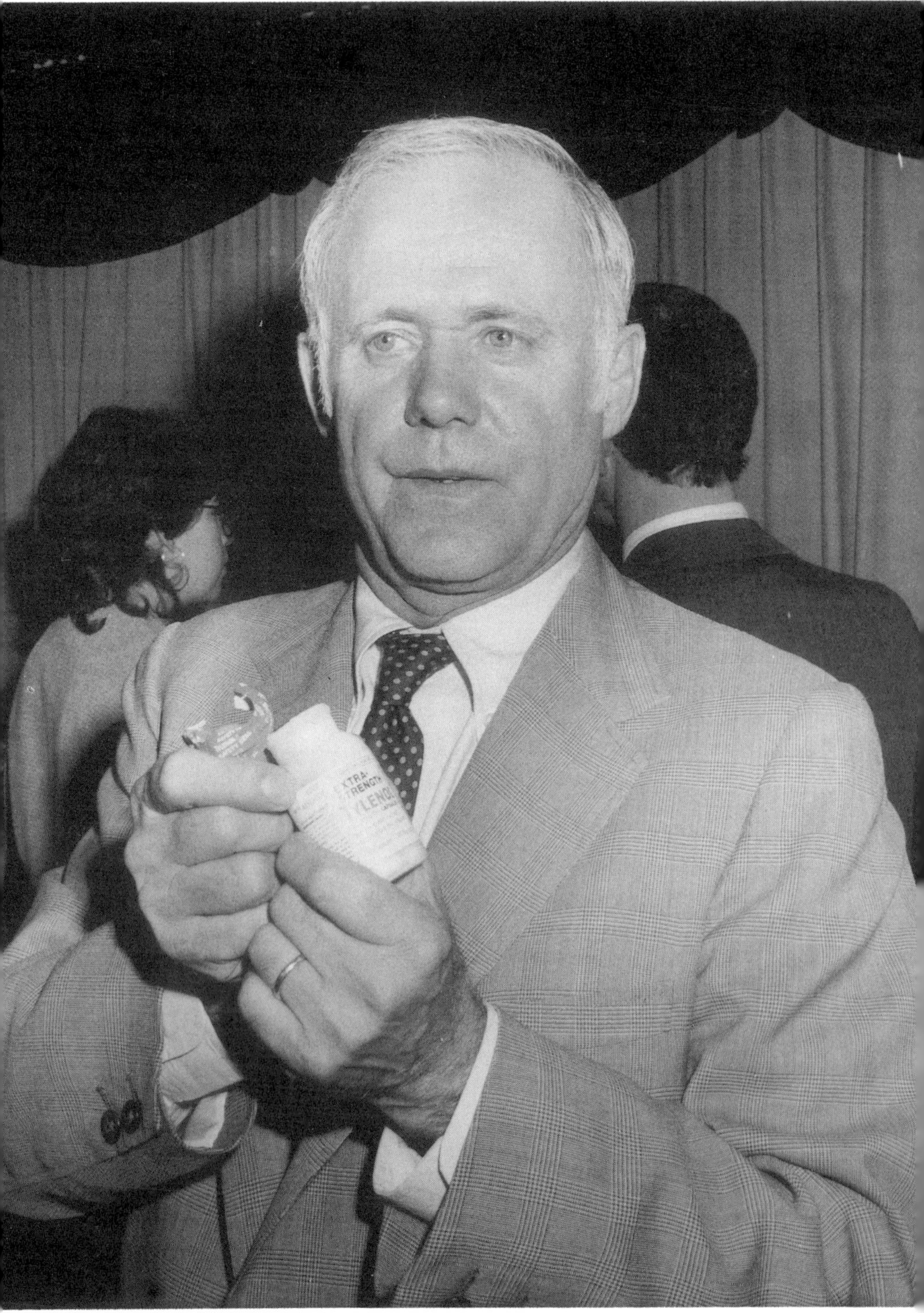
EXTRA-
STRENGTH
YLENOL

Such respect for employees is usually evident in the kind of communication that occurs within the company. Owners and managers understand that they must have information and help that can come only from those who make the product, sell the goods, or deliver the service. Japanese businesses use a system of communication called "quality circles" in which all those involved in the development and production of a product meet regularly to discuss it. Such meetings let everyone know how things are being done and, more important, give everyone an opportunity to contribute to and improve the business. Some companies demonstrate this approach by having everyone wear name tags or address each other by first name regardless of status in the company.

These things put together—attention to high quality and service; belief in the importance of people, either customers or employees; good communication throughout the business—add up to a company's belief that it can be the "best" in a particular area of business. Successful businesses certainly have goals for financial growth and profit, but they talk and think more about the details of doing the job well. The vision of excellence becomes very important to everyone.

Many successful companies are associated with one person. We think of people like Walt Disney, Estée Lauder, and J. Willard Marriott, Sr. These people are very important in establishing the goals of a company—in many cases they actually started the business—but their most important role seems to be their persistent efforts to keep everyone working toward the goals. They keep on keeping on! They are determined to be the best. Their trustworthiness and their willingness to work at whatever needs doing become the means of communicating excellence throughout the business. Achieving excellence becomes a great source of satisfaction for everyone involved. For many people the positive feelings of a job well done and of being part of a great team are more rewarding than money.

James Buske, chairman of Johnson & Johnson Company, demonstrates the new triple-sealed, tamper-resistant package for Tylenol.

SCHOOLS

When we look at the role of excellence in schools, the story is a little different. Nearly all developed countries have laws requiring that children attend school. Everybody has to go. A student may have some choice about whether to attend public, private, or parochial school, but the choices are much more limited than in finding a place to work.

The fact that everyone has to go to school and the way schools develop their programs in light of that requirement have a big influence on their interest in excellence. A school may have one or more of the following goals:

1. To help those students who have the least natural ability to learn basic skills.
2. To give each student the necessary job skills for full employment.
3. To have students learn social skills and be better citizens.
4. To have a certain percentage of students admitted to colleges.

The goals of a school system are complicated even further by the race, language, and economic status of the community. But in a democratic society a school's goals must include clear-cut goals of excellence in academic subject areas regardless of who the students are. What happens in the classroom between teacher and student is the seedbed of democracy.

This relationship between education and freedom is receiving much attention in the United States as evidence mounts that a declining educational level means greater competition from foreign countries. In fact, Thomas Jefferson made that same point in 1816 when he wrote a colleague, "If a nation expects to be ignorant and free, in a state of civilization, it expects what never was and never will be." Having an "edu-

A dedicated teacher with her eighth grade students. They are part of a magnet school specially designated for homeless children.

THINK!
DOORWAYS
DREAMS AND DECISIONS

cated electorate" has always been important. When we let students graduate who can't read, they are not likely to go into the voting booth to read the ballot and vote. The fewer the number of people who vote, the more likely it is that corrupt officeholders will take over or that a nation will be controlled by an outside power. Jefferson had observed this cycle in his own time.

Since the vast majority of schools are supported by public taxes, what the public wants from its schools determines the level of excellence in education. Sometimes the vision of excellence comes from the national level. In a presidential campaign, one candidate said that he wanted to be "the education president." He campaigned on a program to promote and reward educational excellence. This kind of national attention to excellence in the schools starts people thinking and talking about what is happening in their community schools, and the impact can be felt everywhere in the country.

Whether or not national education programs have effect depends on their funding and the commitment from national officials, but it does happen. A recent winner of the Presidential Award for Excellence in Science and Mathematics Teaching received a $7,500 grant from the National Science Foundation. She planned to use the money to build a "Wonder room" at her school, with a wind tunnel for testing model airplanes and equipment for reproducing sound. The motivation provided by the national program will result in exciting learning in a local classroom.

More often it is state and local officials who make the great efforts toward pursuing excellence in the schools. One such effort started in Texas when the state began the "No-pass, no-play" regulation for high school athletes. Football players in Texas, as in many places, enjoy a lot of attention and special privileges, but the state government made it clear that athletes must make the cut in the classroom first.

Almost ten years after being named All-American, Rex Robinson came to the same conclusion. As the star kicker on the 1980 University of Georgia team, his class schedule was carefully planned for him. He cut classes often and enjoyed being a big man on campus, sure that he would be playing pro ball after college. He failed to graduate but did play in the NFL for about two years. Ten years later he began thinking about going back to college. "If you shortchange your education, you're not giving yourself a chance to succeed and excel in the long run," he said.* The way to excellence is sometimes not clear until much time has passed.

Within a community it is often the chamber of commerce or civic club that points out to the school board the importance of excellence. Businesses need employees who are well educated, and the educational system is one of the first things looked at by companies that are thinking about locating in an area.

In this century the major source of support for excellence in schools has come from parents. Until the 1970s such support may have been organized more consistently in parent-teacher associations at local, state, and national levels. Now the variety of parent involvement in school programs is greater. In places as different as Vallejo, California, and Lake George, New York, parents are actually attending school with their children to share the learning experience and to demonstrate that doing well in school is important.

How have your parents supported your school? They have probably paid either property or sales taxes that go for education. If you are in a private school they have paid tuition as well. They have bought clothes, school supplies, books, uniforms, lab fees, lunches. But beyond the financial costs, how have they contributed to the school program? Many parents make regular visits to teachers and principals, volunteer time to help in the library or with special events such as field trips, and spend hours with homework and special projects. The parents' role can be a very large one. Often they tend to do either too much or too little.

Just as one person is often the focal point for the drive for excellence in a business, so one person can lead the way to excellence in a school, and this person is most often the

---

* "The Price of Victory," *U.S. News & World Report*, Jan. 8, 1990.

principal. A woman in Chicago demonstrates that influence well. Grace Dawson, principal of Beethoven Elementary School on Chicago's South Side, knew that many of her students needed more individual help if they were to meet higher standards. She started a Saturday Free School where kids from all the nearby schools are welcome. They work on basic skills and reading comprehension. "We go over every error," she says. "We've got to turn things around."** She has been holding this Saturday school for more than four years, and the kids seem to love it.

Another exciting example of striving for excellence in a school was described in the November 13, 1989, issue of *U.S. News & World Report*. That magazine and IBM have joined to sponsor a program called "To Give & Learn," which honors outstanding teacher-directed student community service programs. Rice High School in the Harlem district of New York was the first winner in the program. The 350 boys who attend the parochial school are mostly black and Hispanic, and from a neighborhood full of drug traffic, bars, boarded-up buildings, and vacant lots piled with trash.

Brother Kenneth Cooper teaches social studies at the school, but not in the usual way. He decided that the ghetto would not overpower his students, that the seniors he taught could make a difference in Harlem by serving the poor, the lonely, and the sick. Following weekly seminars where they discuss and write about social themes such as poverty, injustice, or malnutrition, students must give a certain number of hours to community service. They work in homeless shelters, in AIDS clinics, and in drug rehabilitation centers as tutors to younger students.

That all sounds good enough, but the surprising outcome is that 85 percent of those students go on to college or other additional training after they graduate from Rice. They have caught the vision of excellence that comes from studying to make the most of their own talents while serving the needs of others.

** "Their Grades Improve," *Modern Maturity*, October–November, 1989.

COMMUNITIES

Attacking community problems is often the way people come together to attain high goals or improved standards. In Linn County, Iowa, many bicyclists and picnickers enjoy outings on the Cedar River Nature Trail. The trail, once the route of a trolley line, had been abandoned for some time when the Central Gulf Railroad decided to sell the land. One group of citizens wanted to use the land for recreational purposes; others wanted to purchase it for private use or feared litter and vandals if the land were used for recreation. A nonprofit organization was formed to buy the land, and with the help of a television campaign for support, the recreational interests won out. Now the park is the pride of the area, especially in wildflower season.

It is interesting to see what a community will value and work together to achieve. The media in a community often play an important part in motivating people toward improving a situation. Many towns as small as 12,000 have a local television station, and newspapers have long been the main source of campaigns for change. Two towns, only twenty miles apart, demonstrate their effect. The small daily newspaper in one town covers events thoroughly and accurately. Its editorials call on readers to examine what is happening and often urge the town council to improve situations that are not in the town's best interests. The local paper in the other town is owned by a media chain based several hundred miles away. Its articles are often full of errors, and the editorials generally promote the editor's pet projects or political friends. The levels of community achievement and the reputations of the two towns are directly related to the levels of journalism in the two papers.

Each year various publications rate cities and towns by certain criteria as to living standards and appeal. What makes a good place to live? In a recent issue of *MONEY* magazine one of these lists ranked Bremerton, Washington, at the top. It rated such factors as cleanliness, recreational areas, cost of living, educational standards, crime rate, medical service, and job opportunities. The city has some 180,000 residents, so it is not very large, but it offers many facilities of a city. Try rating your city by the above standards; then ask yourself in what ways it

tries to achieve excellence. What is it especially noted for? Most of us like the place where we live, but we can also suggest some ways to improve it. Perhaps most important, you might try to name the key people who make the difference in your city.

GOVERNMENT

The same rules of excellence apply in the governments of states, provinces, and nations as in communities, schools, and businesses. When a government has a vision of serving its people and improving their way of life, when it works to achieve that vision and gives the people regular opportunity to participate in the government, excellence is sure to follow.

A peculiar fact about governments is that the larger the group or area to be governed, the more important it is to have one responsible, trustworthy person in charge. That kind of person is also essential to lead a government in times of crisis or sharp change.

Fortunately for the human race there have been many such leaders. One who comes to mind is Golda Meir, who served the young state of Israel as its first minister to Moscow in 1948, as minister of labor from 1949 to 1956, minister for foreign affairs from 1956 to 1966, and as prime minister from 1969 to 1974. Golda was born in Kiev, Russia, but in 1906 her family moved to Milwaukee, Wisconsin, where she later taught school. As a young woman she was devoted to the idea of a Jewish state in Palestine, and she responded enthusiastically when David Ben-Gurion came to Milwaukee recruiting people to settle collective farms. In 1921 Golda moved to Palestine, where she was an important part of the birth of Israel following the end of World War II in 1948.

Regardless of the position she held in the Israeli government, she never lost her identification with the people. She

As a leader of her country, Golda Meir was highly respected for her honesty and integrity.

never asked others to shine her shoes or do her laundry; she always traveled tourist class; she often held important government meetings in her kitchen. Above all, she did what had to be done to establish a country and government for the Jewish people. She had retired from government when she was elected prime minister at age seventy. No one doubted her toughness or her honesty. "Golda is the only politician I know who says the same thing in public that she says in private," one official said. Time and again during the troubled days of establishing the new country, this one woman's inspired vision provided the necessary leadership.

Many of the government leaders whom we associate with excellence have lost elections or been discredited at some point in their career. Nonetheless, they established records as persons with the ability to lead and govern. People like Winston Churchill, Harry Truman, and Abraham Lincoln (who lost a total of six elections) fit that description. They did not win every election they entered, but they persisted in giving their best to public service, and they were ready to lead when difficult times came.

Leaders who inspire the citizens of a state toward excellence also have the special talent of communicating well. Of course, history records many leaders who could communicate well and inspire people, but not toward excellence. Adolf Hitler is a good example. Only when a leader backs up inspiring words with responsible deeds do we have excellence.

The world is presently watching the new president of Czechoslovakia, Vaclav Havel, to see how he will lead his country, which was ruled by the Soviets for more than forty years. A playwright and former "enemy of the state" under the communist regime, Havel was unanimously elected by a Parliament including many of the same people who had earlier approved his four-year imprisonment for subversion. Through the years he had continued writing satires about the Communists' rule. The plays earned him enough money to buy a Mercedes-Benz, which he drove every day to his job in a brewery in Prague to which he had been assigned by the government. In spite of being rather shy, he criticized the government on many points and became a hero to people who had had enough of rule by fear.

Whether or not Havel will be a good president remains to be seen, but he has many qualities that suggest he will. He has demonstrated that he wants freedom for his people and that he has the ability to inspire them toward worthy goals. He has personally worked toward those goals for a long time, and his actions match his words.

In his New Year's Day 1990 speech to the Czechoslovakian people, he described the sickness under which they had been living and what must be done:

> "... we have become accustomed to saying one thing and thinking another. We have learned not to believe in anything, not to have consideration for one another and only to look out for ourselves.... But we cannot lay all the blame on those who ruled us before, not only because this would not be true but also because it could detract from the responsibility each of us faces to act on our own freely, sensibly, and quickly.***

He defines the inward requirements of excellence very well!

We have looked at several kinds of groups in this chapter. Although they differ in size, purpose, structure, and makeup, they have some common factors when it comes to excellence. For a group or organization to seek excellence, it must have a shared vision of what is best, and all members must bend their efforts and talents toward that goal. Communication within the group must be clear and based on respect for the members. Morale is high, and there is a feeling of trust in the leadership and the goals. Quite often one individual in the group brings the vision and effort that tip the scales toward excellence.

We cannot always control the communities or groups to which we belong. We cannot choose the nation or community in which we are born and live as children. We rarely choose the school where we start our education and begin learning the basics of education. We usually have some choice about our

---

*** Quoted in "The Word as Arrow," *U.S. News & World Report*, Feb 26, 1990.

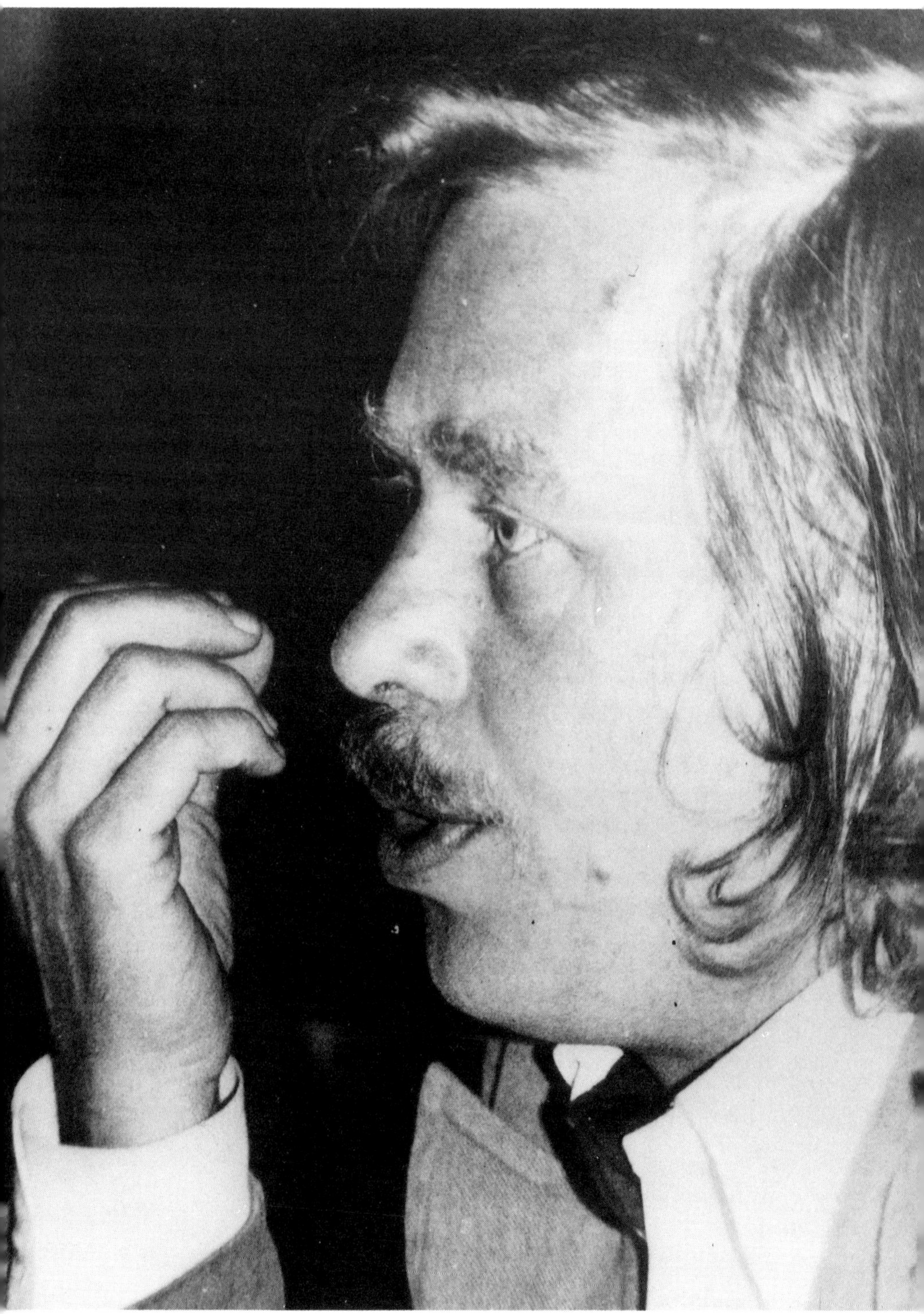

job situation. Regardless of where we find ourselves, we can be sure of one thing: "if the organization or group cherishes high standards, the behavior of the individuals who enter it is inevitably influenced." So wrote John W. Gardner in *Excellence; Can We Be Equal and Excellent Too?* It does matter who we hang out with. They will influence us with their values and goals. The obvious thing is to look for groups with the traits of excellence.

We cannot close without putting the shoe on the other foot. Each of us also has an influence on the groups of which we are part. We have the opportunity to become that person with the vision and effort that makes the difference for all the rest. Excellence is a two-way street.

Vaclav Havel, as seen in 1977 during his younger, dissident days.

CHAPTER 10

The View at the Top

In the song "Imagine," John Lennon gives us his vision of a world free of war and poverty. The images he suggests with his words stay in our minds along with the haunting melody. Lennon understood the power within each of us to create new realities springing from imagination.

We often associate imagination with the childhood years. Children imagine monsters under the bed, make-believe friends and animals. They imagine that they are adults when they play with toys and dolls. They create all sorts of imaginary settings in their games.

Creative artists continue to rely on imagination as the source of their work as adults. Writers and storytellers imagine their plots and characters. Dancers imagine moves to fit the music. Sculptors and painters imagine the forms and colors of their art. The great Italian sculptor Michelangelo Buonarroti was barely twenty years old when he "saw" the figure of Mary holding her crucified Son Jesus within a massive block of marble. The stone was considered unfit for carving, but Michelangelo had a vision. Starting in 1496, he chiseled for several years to release the larger-than-life figures that continue to awe visitors in St. Peter's Cathedral in Rome.

Even though we may lack the artistic talent of a Michelangelo, imagination can work for us as well. It can provide us with an exciting vision of what we want to become. Imagine that you are relaxing in your favorite spot on the first day after your retirement from a successful career about fifty years from now. You have been asked to give an interview for the local cable network, and the interviewer's first question is, "What was the high point of your career?" You must look back on your life and describe the accomplishment of which you are most proud.

Think about that for a few minutes and write down the images and words that come to you. Whatever you imagine is a very good clue to what you really want to accomplish. Group experiments with this game show that more than eighty percent of the people who try it can give rather specific answers. In fact, it seems easier than looking forward from the present and setting goals based on what we think we want to do.

There are many ways of thinking about setting goals for what we want to become. The philosopher Alfred North Whitehead summed up the goals of human beings as follows:

"Man wants to live.
Man wants to live better.
Man wants to live even better."

Although we may agree with his thought as a general statement about mankind, it does not give us much of a specific image for a satisfying and successful life.

The idea of success and worthwhile goals has changed over the years. In the United States, Benjamin Franklin is regarded as the first writer about success. Born in 1706 as the fifteenth child of a Boston soap and candlemaker, he excelled in four fields: statesman, inventor, author, and scientist. Franklin believed that success and satisfaction in life came from character. Traits such as hard work, frugality, honesty, and loyalty were the stuff from which success came. Franklin's wise and witty sayings supporting that view are still quoted; sayings such as, "Early to bed and early to rise makes a man healthy, wealthy, and wise," and "God helps them that help themselves."

In later years the people who wrote about success thought

ALL YOU NEED IS LOVE
GIVE PEACE A CHANCE

personality was more important. A person needed magnetism and sparkle and a good public image in order to "win friends and influence people" as the title of Dale Carnegie's still-popular book says. It was important to speak well and to say positive things. That view evolved into the notion that positive thinking is critical to success. A person must believe that he or she is going to make it. The winners in life are the ones with winning personalities and winning attitudes.

Recently, some writers have defined success more in terms of the power a person has to make things happen. Life is viewed as a struggle in which getting ahead calls for being shrewd, outwitting other people, and making money. People who seem to have a lot to spend, especially on a lavish life-style, are considered "successful." We are seeing some examples, however, that prove that money and power have only a short-term connection with success.

In fact, all these views of success have some elements of truth. And at any given time there are many views of success and how to achieve it. In 1986, George Gallup, Jr., and Alec M. Gallup published the results of an extensive survey of successful people in the United States: *The Great American Success Story: Factors That Affect Achievement.* They interviewed and sent questionnaires to 1,500 people listed in *Who's Who in America* on their personal traits, family background, education, outside interests, and experience in the fields where they had reached the top.

The answers varied a great deal, but they agreed strongly that hard work and the desire to excel were the most important factors contributing to their success. They also agreed that the least important factors were family background and the desire for material possessions and money. The rewards of success mentioned most often were "recognition by peers" and "being able to contribute to society."

One of those interviewed was John Marks Templeton, notable investor and developer of many investment opportunities including the Templeton Growth Fund. In describing his view of success, Templeton emphasizes that all his assets and talents

A fan remembers the hopes and dreams of a better world inspired by the songs of John Lennon.

were given to him by others and by God. In turn he feels that he is responsible for managing those gifts or assets for the good of all. He considers his success measured by the degree to which he helps others as he helps himself.

We can conclude that success, like excellence, does not have one generally accepted definition. Both carry the meaning of being outstanding or having reached the top in some field of achievement. And both have an outer and an inner measure. In the outer or objective sense, a person is evaluated by others; in the inner or subjective sense, the person uses his or her own feelings about personal value and qualities to decide whether excellence and success have been reached.

However, there is general agreement on one point regardless of who is judging: What a person does makes a difference. Each person has some form of excellence within that seeks expression through words and actions. All of us have value, and we have the power to change ourselves and our world for the better. A new book entitled *Living Philosophies: The Reflections of Some Eminent Men and Women of Our Time* quotes Jane Goodall, the woman who has spent years studying chimpanzees, as saying that even among the animals the influence of certain individuals is apparent. "It is impossible to overemphasize the power of the individual on the shaping of the values of a society."

Thus we each create our definition of excellence. We may look to models for inspiration, but the final picture that emerges from within is unique. Let your imagination "play" with your experiences to give you a clearer vision of what you can be and do.

You can capture the meaning of excellence with pictures or analogies. For example, you might picture striving to achieve excellence to be like herding cattle into a corral. First you work one side of the herd and then the other, keeping your rope ready to lasso any strays as you move the group of animals toward the gate. You count on your horse to obey your commands on the bridle, and perhaps you have a dog to help with the roundup. You rely on your experience in other roundups, and you keep moving the herd toward the gate. Your goal is clear.

The story brings to mind pictures we have seen in Western

Jane Goodall recognized the value of the individual to society in her unique studies of the wild chimpanzee.

movies. When we relate it to the pursuit of excellence, it also communicates certain ideas about how much effort is involved, how many different things you have to think about and watch for, and how you have to rely on others for help. Maybe it also calls to mind the satisfied grin on the cowpuncher's face as he closes the gate after all the cattle are inside.

Or we might say that achieving excellence is like using a mirror. You know you need to check your hair and clothes as you dress each day, so you go to a store to purchase a new mirror. But if you go to an antique store, you may find all the mirrors are worn or cracked. Your reflection will have gaps or spots in it where the silver has worn off the back of the mirror. If you go to a novelty store, you will find only distorting mirrors like the ones in the fun house at carnivals. Your reflection will be too short or tall or fat or thin. Neither of those mirrors will serve the purpose you have in mind because they do not reflect an honest image.

That comparison calls up many images, from looking in your mirror at home each day to looking in a mirror at a carnival. Those mental pictures help you understand that getting a true picture of yourself is very important in excellence, and you want a true picture so you can know your best qualities and use them in satisfying ways.

Or we could say that striving for excellence is like going to Disney World for the day. You can't wait to get there and ride the thriller rides and see the shows and then watch the fireworks at night. As it turns out, you get to do all those things but only by standing in line for most of the day. That is pretty boring, but it's the only way to enjoy what you came for. The parable's relation to excellence is obvious. Striving for the highest level in any area of life has a lot of plain boring routine hours when you must keep on doing what has to be done to reach your goal. But when you get there the fireworks are great!

Each of these comparisons illustrates one or more of the basic points we have been discussing throughout this book:

Self-confidence
Integrity
Respect for others
Persistence

Those four points are like the four points of a compass. We take our direction from them as we walk the road to excellence. They give us the clear vision of being the best.

It should be clear at this point that excellence does not come in a day or a month or perhaps even in a year. The recognition of our achievement or the inner satisfaction may be a long time coming. But as we stay on course, the pictures in our minds are very important. To use another comparison, we can say that working for personal excellence is sometimes like looking through a kaleidoscope. Only you can see the beautiful patterns of color at the end of the tube, but you do not doubt the reality of what you see just because others do not see it at that time.

Alice in Wonderland by Lewis Carroll is a book of many

unusual visions and conversations between strange creatures. One of those conversations takes place between Alice and the Queen when Alice is most discouraged:

"There's no use trying," she said: "one *can't* believe impossible things."

"I daresay you haven't had much practice," said the Queen. "When I was your age, I always did it for half-an-hour a day. Why, sometimes I've believed as many as six impossible things before breakfast."

The Queen obviously practiced making her visions come true. Only you can hold onto the vision of excellence that you have for yourself, no matter how impossible it may seem to others.

In the southeastern corner of Tennessee is a mountain only 2,126 feet high, but it is so situated that from its top on a clear day one can see seven states. It is appropriately named Lookout Mountain. Many people go to the top and turn toward all directions until they have seen all the states. A viewer feels a sense of wonder and mastery at being able to view so much territory without traveling.

That sense of being a lookout is close to the definition of excellence we mentioned in Chapter 1. Excellence is being on top, having reached a high level, being in a position to have the far view and see things in all directions, perhaps even to tell your friends what lies beyond. It is the vision of excellence.

Bibliography

Books

Bellah, Robert N.; Madsen, Richard; Sullivan, William M., *et al.* *Habits of the Heart: Individualism and Commitment in American Life*. New York: Harper, 1985.

Davidson, Margaret. *The Golda Meir Story*. New York: Scribner's, 1976.

Duckmeyer, Lowell A., and Humphreys, Martha. *Winning and Losing*. New York: Franklin Watts, 1984.

Downey, Glanville. *Aristotle: Dean of Early Science*. New York: Franklin Watts, 1962.

Furse, Margaret Lewis. *Nothing But the Truth?* Nashville: Abingdon Press, 1981.

Gallup, George Jr. and Alec M. *The Great American Success Story: Factors That Affect Achievement*. Homewood, IL: Dow Jones-Irwin, 1986.

Gardner, John W. *Excellence,* rev. ed. New York: W. W. Norton, 1984.

Goertzel, Victor and Mildred G. *Cradles of Eminence*. Boston: Little Brown, 1962.

Haldane, Bernard. *Career Satisfaction and Success: A Guide to Job Freedom*. New York: American Management Association, 1974.

Hughes, Riley. *How to Write Creatively.* New York: Franklin Watts, 1980.

Kirschenbaum, Howard; Napier, Rodney; and Simon, Sidney B. *Wad-ja-Get? The Grading Game in American Education.* New York: Hart Publishing Company, 1971.

Kohn, Alfie. *No Contest: The Case Against Competition.* Boston: Houghton, Mifflin, 1986.

Lang, Binny and Chris. *Your Future Success: A Student's Guide to Effective Study.* Melbourne: Ashwood House, 1990.

Malvern, Gladys. *Dancing Star: The Story of Anna Pavlova.* New York: Julian Messner, 1942.

Miller, Stephen. *Excellence and Equity: The National Endowment for the Humanities.* Lexington: University Press of Kentucky, 1984.

Parker, Don H. *Schooling for Individual Excellence.* New York: Thomas Nelson & Sons, 1963.

Peck, M. Scott. *The Different Drum: Community Making and Peace.* New York: Simon & Schuster, 1987.

Peters, Thomas J., and Waterman, Robert H., Jr. *In Search of Excellence.* New York: Warner Books, 1982.

Selsam, Millicent E. *The Quest of Captain Cook,* illus. Lee J. Ames. Garden City: Doubleday, 1962.

Shelton, Charles M. *Morality and the Adolescent: A Pastoral Psychology Approach.* New York: Crossroad, 1989.

Smedes, Lewis B. *Choices: Making Right Decisions in a Complex World.* San Francisco: Harper, 1986.

Tchudi, Stephen. *The Young Learner's Handbook.* New York: Scribner's, 1987.

Toynbee, Arnold J. *A Study of History.* Abridgment of Vols. I-VI by D. C. Somervell. New York: Oxford University Press, 1947.

Waxler, Myer, and Wolf, Robert L. *Good-Bye Job, Hello Me.* Chicago: Scott Foresman, 1987.

Periodicals

Allman, William F., et al. "The Best of America: The U.S. News Survey." *U.S. News & World Report,* July 9, 1990, pp. 43–78.

Brophy, Beth, and Goode, Erica E. "Amazing Families." *U.S. News & World Report*, Dec. 12, 1988, pp. 78–87.

Chesnoff, Richard Z. "The Prisoner Who Took the Castle." *U.S. News & World Report*, Feb. 26, 1990, pp. 33–37.

Cox, G. A. "A Prescription for Excellence." *Vital Speeches of the Day* (54: 566–9), July 1, 1988.

Humphrey, Nancy. "The Genius from the Hills." *Nashville Scene*, July 12, 1990, pp. 14–18.

Ross, Steven. "Rethinking Thinking." *Modern Maturity*, February-March, 1990, pp. 52–58.

Sanoff, Alvin P. "Nothing Sells Like Success." *U.S. News & World Report*, Sept. 10, 1990, p. 82.

Sanoff, Alvin P. with Joannie M. Schrof. "The Price of Victory." *U.S. News & World Report*, Jan. 8, 1990, pp. 44–50.

Index

NEW HANOVER COUNTY PUBLIC LIBRARY